RETHINKING
SUCCESS

RETHINKING
SUCCESS

*Eight Essential Practices for
Finding Meaning in Work and Life*

J. Douglas Holladay

HarperOne
An Imprint of HarperCollins*Publishers*

HarperOne

RETHINKING SUCCESS. Copyright © 2020 by J. Douglas Holladay. All rights reserved. Printed in the United States of America. No part of this book may be used or reproduced in any manner whatsoever without written permission except in the case of brief quotations embodied in critical articles and reviews. For information, address HarperCollins Publishers, 195 Broadway, New York, NY 10007.

HarperCollins books may be purchased for educational, business, or sales promotional use. For information, please email the Special Markets Department at SPsales@harpercollins.com.

FIRST EDITION

Designed by Terry McGrath

Library of Congress Cataloging-in-Publication Data is available upon request.

ISBN 978-0-06-289788-6

20 21 22 23 24   LSC   10 9 8 7 6 5 4 3 2 1

This book is dedicated to Ry, Hays, and Kempe, three young men whom I love and admire.

Carpe Diem.

The real voyage of discovery consists not in seeking new landscapes but in having new eyes.

—MARCEL PROUST

Contents

Introduction

"The problem with getting everything is you run out of reasons to keep trying."

"People who made sudden success are telling me this is normal and will pass. That's good to know! I guess I'll take a shower then!"

"Hanging out in Ibiza with a bunch of friends and partying with famous people, able to do whatever I want, and I've never felt more isolated."

"When we sold the company, the biggest effort went into making sure the employees got taken care of, and they all hate me now."

These are among the many tweets of Markus Persson, who in 2014, at age thirty-five, sold his wildly popular company, Minecraft, for $2.5 billion. He quickly purchased a 23,000-square-foot mansion in the Hollywood hills for $70 million. He was living the dream, right? Hardly. He was depressed and lonely, an emotional state that became widely shared throughout the Twitterverse.

So why our fascination with the pain and foibles of people like Markus Persson? In many ways he represents our wildest dreams of success come true. What would happen if we found ourselves billionaires? How could that not make us feel fulfilled and happy?

And yet we are not surprised to hear that success often fails to bring happiness. Why does success leave some feeling isolated, lonely, and unhappy?

As it turns out, Persson's experience is not uncommon. Many find themselves hugely successful but failing at life. As it turns out, success without also maintaining a larger sense of purpose and meaning leaves many feeling adrift and alone. We are creatures who crave meaning in our lives, and without it we lose our moorings.

Researchers find that people have meaningful lives when three conditions are met: first, their lives make sense; second, their lives are driven by purpose; and, third, they are a part of something much bigger than themselves.[1] I would add a fourth condition, one that is implicit in the three above: they maintain rich human connection.

This is a book about the illusive notion of success and how the very things we do to attain it can prove counterproductive and vacuous in the end. Ironically, the chase itself, as in Markus Persson's case, is frequently more satisfying than the realization of the sought-after prize. In my view, Persson has a teachable moment, just now, where he will either self-destruct or discover a richer, deeper existence. To go up, most of us must first go down. Yet it's quite unsettling to stand in this naked light. Finding a purpose requires paying attention in those dark moments when clarity and a true epiphany await. You can continue to avoid the truth about yourself for a time, but not indefinitely. So let me tell you about Ted.

Ted Leonsis is a friend, a hugely successful entrepreneur, and owner of four professional sports teams, including the Washington Wizards and the Caps. At an age even younger than Persson, Leonsis had a moment of clarity when he decided what truly mattered. Here is the story he told me:

It was 1984. I was twenty-seven years old and had recently sold for $60 million an early New Media company that I'd built. And then in fulfillment of the randomness of life, I got on the wrong plane. A routine flight from Melbourne, Florida, to Atlanta ended with an emergency landing. No one was hurt, but in the thirty-five minutes that we spent unsure of whether the landing gear was going to work, circling the airport, burning off fuel, and learning how to brace for a crash landing, I had to face up to something I really didn't like: if that plane crashed, I wouldn't die happy.

It was a reckoning, a wake-up call. I had all the toys money could buy. At a ridiculously young age, I had achieved what we all believe is the American Dream, and for a poor kid from Brooklyn, it had all seemed to come easy. But I wasn't happy. It was the most important discovery of my life. The moment I got off that plane, with shaking knees and a queasy stomach, I resolved to pursue happiness and live my life without regret. I was given the world's all-time greatest mulligan, the gift of a second chance to live my life properly.

Two lives, two opportunities to discover purpose and meaning. One used his "moment" to alter the trajectory of his life—toward greater meaning—while the other feels lost. Henry David Thoreau describes the life leading up to this crisis moment as "quiet desperation," while T. S. Eliot warns of the risk of becoming "hollow men."

You might find yourself at a similar turning point. Perhaps your sense of emptiness is hidden from others, and yet you know it intimately: the late night wonderings, wanting to feel alive and connected, often numbing the pain in ways we all understand too well. On some level, we understand there is a choice: continue on this path of emptiness or probe deeper to discover some real purpose and meaning in life.

These concepts can seem terribly remote and philosophical, yet they actually occupy much of our thinking. *New York Times* columnist and friend David Brooks sharpens the distinction between a life of meaning and one of hollow striving when he juxtaposes our "résumé virtues" (our concrete accomplishments) with our "eulogy virtues" (character strengths people would lift up at our funeral) in his March 2014 TED

Talk.[2] This distinction is useful as we examine our behavior and how we expend our energies. Although accomplishments are satisfying for a time, they eventually leave us empty and unfulfilled if not attached to some larger purpose. The eulogy virtues feed our sense of well-being and contribution to the greater good. We derive our senses of meaning and purpose from them.

Purpose consists of the central motivating aims of our life—the reason we arise in the morning. Purpose guides life decisions, influences behaviors, shapes goals, offers a sense of direction, and fosters meaning. If we are fortunate, our purpose is tied to our vocation, and we find meaning in satisfying work. Meaning pertains to the significance of living in general; we believe our lives count for something and involve serving, creating, and connecting with others.

Meaning and purpose might be easy to define, but figuring out how they apply to our lives is not always easy; neither is maintaining them. I've structured this book around eight practices that I believe reside at the heart of a meaningful life of thriving.

Offering clear answers seems a necessary response to the urgency of the moment, but I find the discipline of asking ourselves questions demands that we learn to enjoy the journey as well. It is not a quick fix. Arriving at the destination of true meaning involves, in my view, considering the right questions. "Never stop questioning," Albert Einstein famously urged. Harvard Business School professor Alison

Wood Brooks explains why asking questions can be a powerful practice: "The wellspring of all questions is wonder and curiosity and a capacity for delight."[3] Rather than limiting choices, as searching for "right" answers frequently does, questions enlarge the field of possibility.

Questions suggest a longer period of discovery during which rich clues and insights appear along the way and worm their way into our hearts and minds. Answers sometimes change, while the questions remain relevant. European poet Rainer Maria Rilke sheds light on why living with questions is valuable: "Have patience with everything unresolved in your heart and try to love the questions themselves. . . . Live the questions now. Perhaps then, someday far in the future, you will gradually, without even noticing it, live your way into the answer."[4]

After four decades of working closely with leaders, observing them and listening to their deepest thoughts and concerns, I have distilled the pursuit of meaning and purpose into eight practices. These lessons have been gleaned from interactions and probing conversations with colleagues at the White House, the State Department, and Goldman Sachs; the bright MBA students in my classes at Georgetown; private CEO clients I have coached; and other leaders struggling to find greater purpose.

Although much of this book is grounded in solid research, its real value departs from the message of those who have spent their lives within the ivy-covered walls of academia. As

Hamilton famously sang, I have been "in the room," up close and personal, in a front-row seat to the action. The perspective or worldview that has emerged over these years of close exposure is captured in these practices that facilitate finding a meaningful life path. They are intended to be practical rather than theoretical. If you take these eight to heart and translate them into real life, you will thrive in work as well as in life.

The eight practices are:

1. Know and live your own story, rather than fulfilling someone else's dreams and expectations for you.
2. Maintain deep connections in your core relationships, rather than assuming they will take care of themselves or they don't matter.
3. Regularly express gratitude, rather than taking good things for granted and only focusing on worries and problems.
4. Learn to forgive and serve, rather than falling into the trap of believing your life is only about the wrongs done to you.
5. Define success and failure for yourself, rather than allowing your worth to be defined by others' shifting and subjective standards.
6. Make sure risk continues to play a role in your life, rather than allowing the torpor of security to deaden your soul.

7. Integrate your life, rather than compartmentalizing it.
8. Work to leave a legacy for others, rather than being stuck in the small and limited world of self-focus.

My hope is that the practice of regularly asking questions of yourself regarding these eight core themes will aid you in embracing what Aristotle called *eudaimonia*, human flourishing, a life rich with true success and purpose and undergirded with meaning.

— 1 —

The Illusions of Success

After I finished some early ventures in politics and diplomacy, I decided to figure out what was next for me. While exploring a new career in investment banking, I met with a banker from Morgan Stanley in his lush office in midtown Manhattan. To all appearances, he embodied success, but ever since that day I have been haunted by our exchange, never forgetting what he confessed. After a spirited hour-long interview, he paused, choosing his words carefully.

"You have had an amazing eclectic career. It has been full of adventure and contribution." He leaned forward and quietly continued, "I'm in prison. It's a very nice prison, but one nonetheless. I have put career above all else and destroyed three marriages, and I'm alienated from my oldest son. I have everything but feel trapped and alone. How did I get here?"

His honest reflection was punctuated by the right question: "How did I get here?" His feelings of emptiness and regret were real. What was less clear was the way forward.

And then there's Gloria Nelund, who was CEO of one of the largest global-wealth management companies in the world. Her husband was raising their special-needs child in San Diego while Gloria pursued her demanding job. She was absent for extended periods, a reality that weighed heavily on her. But hers was a high-class problem in her rarefied world. And then a pivotal day arrived. Gloria had just closed the biggest deal of her career. She was surrounded by lawyers and investment bankers applauding her smarts and strategic sense.

But as she was leaving the closing meeting, a stark realization swept over this talented leader: she had no one to celebrate the biggest accomplishment of her career with; she was successful yet utterly alone. She concluded that it was an empty victory. But she chose not to remain in her prison. She resigned the following week and found work that enabled her to fashion a life that included those things that were important to her.

When I consider stories like those of Nelund and the Morgan Stanley banker, I ponder how many other leaders feel isolated, lonely, and trapped. Oddly enough, we rarely understand the illusion of success until we achieve some. Robert A. Burton, former chief of neurology at UC–San Francisco's Medical Center at Mount Zion, offers real insight: "We readily recognize meaning by its absence."[1] It's often in the attainment of the prize that we understand its limitations.

And if the shocking disappointment with achieving

success were not enough, there's "imposter phenomenon," known also as "imposter syndrome." Psychotherapist Pauline Clance first described it in 1985 as a feeling that your "achievements are undeserved and the worry that they are likely to be exposed as a fraud."[2] Such feelings only contribute to a sense of unworthiness, emptiness, and solitude. We all have been there.

Have the Lights Gone Out?

When I teach my Georgetown MBA class, I pose an awkward question: "How many of you would say the lights have gone out for your parents, particularly for your father?" I explain what I mean. Simply put, their parents have few real friends, have little passion for anything, lack purpose, and seem adrift. Essentially, they are experiencing what the seventeenth-century French philosopher Blaise Pascal refers to as a vacuum in the heart. Typically, over half the students in my class raise their hands; the others perhaps want to, yet out of loyalty resist the urge.

Then I explain that the purpose of my class is to offer practical tools and strategies for life, so that the students' own children, taking a similar course one day, would not have to raise their hands. With that, the energy in the room soars. They seem eager to discover that elusive path to keeping the lights on throughout their lives.

The most recent data from the National Center for Health Statistics suggests that suicide rates among men between the ages of forty-five and sixty-four increased 43 percent between 1999 and 2014.[3] And unlike women, who seem to connect in ways unimaginable to most men, men often lack the ability to reflect and disclose their pain and feelings of isolation. Still, few of us are taught to explore the deeply human matters that are at the core of who we are. Our identities are typically tied to what we do rather than who we are. The result can be feeling lost, which often leads to poor choices.

Harvard business professor Clayton Christensen observed that none of his former students set out with the intent to destroy their marriage, become alienated from their children, commit suicide, or even end up in jail. Yet many of his students found themselves there, broken and alone, wondering.[4] We are taught to chase success and assume everything else will take care of itself. That is not how life actually works.

The nineteenth surgeon general of the United States, Vivek Murthy, identified the central health risk of our time, one far greater than even obesity or smoking, as loneliness. In 2017 Murthy wrote: "Today, over 40 percent of adults in America report feeling lonely, and research suggests that the real number may well be higher."[5] My friend Rob Kaplan, former Harvard Business School professor and now president and CEO of the Dallas Fed, characterized many leaders he knew in his book *What You're Really Meant to Do*: "I am constantly struck by how isolated people are, despite being hyperconnected on Facebook or closely followed on Twitter. In my experience, one of the key impediments to reaching our potential is isolation."[6]

Robert Putnam, in his classic work *Bowling Alone*, was an early whistle-blower for the alarming and growing disconnection between people across our nation, viewing the demise of bowling leagues and the sparse attendance at PTA meetings as evidence of the fraying social fabric of our society. Nineteenth-century historian Alexis de Tocqueville, in observing the inherent strength of our young nation, saw local societies and groupings of all sorts as vital to our social and national strength. The shift toward solitude is real and urgent and has everything to do with our crisis of meaning.

Detective Sergeant Ashley Jones, with the Avon and Somerset Police in England, was shocked at a fraud victim's response to the crime committed against her. The victim, an elderly woman, would get a daily call from a gentleman pretending to be her friend. He eventually persuaded her to give him $31,000. Her response when Jones asked why she sent the con man money was surprising: "Otherwise, I would never speak to another person for weeks on end." Very dear, but so sad.

Inspector Jones decided to do something about the profound loneliness among the elderly in his area of western England. In local parks, several benches were designated "chat benches." He urged locals to sit awhile and converse with others. The simple idea caught on and worked wonderfully.

People began connecting. There are now more than forty such benches scattered throughout the United Kingdom.[7]

In 2010, with the encouragement of friends, I started Path-North, an initiative to help often-isolated leaders to "broaden their definitions of success" to include meaning and human connection. We gather regularly to discuss what the Greeks referred to as "the good life," a life of thriving with purpose at its core. One of our initial PathNorth trips was aboard the fabled Orient Express train in Europe. Yet we did it a bit differently. We called it the Magical Mystery Tour and brought magicians along with us.

But the lasting impact stemmed from what occurred at night when we discussed what matters in life. In keeping with the magic motif, I posed two questions: "What are the illusions you had about life?" and "What are the mysteries you are still trying to figure out?" These leaders shared deeply and, even now, continue to feel connected ten years later. There is an intense hunger for genuine community where people feel related in truly human ways.

Only if we establish and maintain genuine human relationships can we avoid the dangerous illusions about success.

Real and Vulnerable

In my midtwenties, I met the Democratic senator from Iowa Harold Hughes. Harold became a close and trusted friend, though he intimidated me greatly. To say he was bigger than life was a gross understatement. He had a commanding presence, due in part to his deep baritone voice and stocky physique. He had been a hard-drinking, chain-smoking tough guy who decided he just might make a difference in public service.

With his colorful language and straight talk, he was an atypical senator. He had been a truck driver, with limited formal education, who became the governor of Iowa and then a US senator and finally ran for the presidency. While running for governor, he was known to have said, "My opponent has charged that I have been in jail in four states for drunkenness and disorderly conduct. That's a damn lie. I was in jail in six states."

Hughes won election after election by a landslide. Why? Because he was so incredibly real. By sharing his flaws so openly and vulnerably, he became "everyman," and people loved him for it. The public knew him as a flesh-and-blood human rather than a celluloid, perfectly scripted politician. They might choose to disagree with his liberal politics, but Iowans loved his gruff straight talk and honest manner.

Don't you feel similarly drawn to what's real in others? People don't want others to be perfect; they are attracted to those who are authentic and true to who they are. The key to long-lasting and meaningful human connections is to find those with whom we can be genuine and vulnerable.

So much wasted energy is expended living up to what

Trappist monk and spiritual writer Thomas Merton described as the "perceived greatness of others." A friend recently said to me, "Never compare your insides with another's outside." We all seem to think that others have it together and we are the outlier, the messed-up one. This simply is not the case. We all have our shadow sides and demons to tame.

Once, when I was on the White House staff, Mother Teresa came to my office. In a feeble effort to make small talk I asked this remarkable saint, "So what's it like actually being Mother Teresa?" All of a sudden she got still and focused and said, "The longer I live, the more I realize that I am capable of any sin." We all are trying to figure it out and live true to who we are.

After suggesting to one of my Georgetown classes that our point of identity with others is not our polished image and accomplishments but rather our broken parts and dark sides, a hand shot up in the front row.

"Professor, I would like to say something. I have lived with a debilitating stutter that drove me to a lonely existence. And while I thrived academically, I had no friends and existed in a small world, alone. By sophomore year in college, I decided that I had cried enough. Life was not worth the effort if this was to be my lot. I decided to end my life. But before I did, I would do something vulnerable, something I had never contemplated doing: engage with others and let them see up close my disability. Unbelievably, the more I engaged, the less I stuttered. They even began to share their own fears and vulnerabilities. And guess what else, professor?" He paused for dramatic effect. "I am president of my Georgetown MBA class, and I give public speeches regularly."

His words were met with a pregnant silence. Noting a teachable moment and being the smart-ass I am, I said to the class, "So Clark has revealed an amazing story, a painful passage from fear and isolation to a new beginning. But you are winners. Clark here has revealed a serious flaw. How many of you during the break want to go to the registrar's office and transfer from this class? Raise your hands."

Of course, no hands went up. Then I posed the more important question: "How many of you feel safer because of what Clark shared?" All hands shot high.

The things we loathe about ourselves and hide from others can be the very things that connect us in true relationship and community. To chance being real, as Clark did, requires boldly moving from our comfort zone and allowing others to really know us. If we are willing to be vulnerable, we do not need to remain isolated and imprisoned.

One of the true rock stars of medical science is my friend Francis Collins, director of the National Institutes of Health. In that capacity he is the leading medical personality in the nation. If that were not enough, Francis earlier led the Human Genome Project, which landed him on the cover of *TIME* magazine. This groundbreaking project mapped the human genome, a feat that promised to revolutionize medical science and practice. When asked how he felt leading such a prestigious institution with staggering responsibilities and promise, he simply said, "I was a bit insecure about whether I really was qualified to lead something of this magnitude, and a little uneasy about revealing the things that I didn't know."[8]

If Francis Collins feels inadequate, then we should not be ashamed to admit our own insecurities. At the same time, aren't we drawn to such humility, to those who have the quiet confidence to disclose their weaknesses? And aren't we repelled and mistrustful of bravado and naked ego? They seem so dishonest.

Creating a Safe Place for Questions

Only later in life did I realize that my fascination with questions of meaning and purpose was a bit unusual. My father introduced me early on to Socrates and his notion that "the unexamined life was not worth living." My dad was an atheist, brought to this position by his disappointing experience with religious practice in the small Southern town of Union, Mississippi. He lived and died searching for clues to what Freud called "the riddle of life." When I read "The Hound of Heaven," by the nineteenth-century English poet Francis Thompson, with its images of God's relentless efforts to relate to us, it seemed to capture my father's complicated relationship with God and belief.

My father's mistrust of organized religion and faith influenced my own views and where not to search for answers. So imagine his mix of emotions when, at eighteen, I informed him that I had become a follower of Jesus. His only context for understanding my direction was his disappointing experience with a religious practice characterized by judgmentalism and fear of open inquiry.

Nonetheless, I am my father's son. In a way, I still bring his skeptical eye to matters of faith and discussions of meaning. My faith has only deepened my commitment to exploring questions. My life mission has been to create safe spaces for honest inquiry about what truly matters. So faith for me has enlarged my world and made me eager to engage others who are different. I am certain that, in some subconscious way, I am creating places where my father's inquiring mind would have been welcomed. Perhaps what makes my approach unique are the nontraditional places where I have brought conversations about meaning into the mix, such as in the White House, the State Department, Goldman Sachs, various board rooms, and elsewhere in the broader business community.

I was once asked when I first spoke about questions of meaning with a business leader. I recall it vividly. It was during the second semester of my freshman year of college. I was nineteen and a volunteer leader of a youth group in Durham, North Carolina. A call came from the wife of the congressman from nearby Raleigh. She was effusively thanking me for helping her niece through a difficult adolescent challenge. She clearly overstated my role, but it felt good to be thanked.

She then paused and asked me about another matter. The most prominent business owner in the region was going through a real crisis. Might I help? I agreed to meet with G.P., unsure what I might have to offer a man my father's age. Yet for the next two months G.P. drove his splendid Mercedes to Chapel Hill for conversation. I would sit uncomfortably in the passenger seat as he poured out his problems, mostly related to inheriting great wealth, his failing marriage, and feelings of worthlessness. Finally after many sessions, I looked at this wounded man and explained awkwardly that I had unfortunately exhausted my ability to help. I felt like a failure.

By this time, due to the despair that enveloped him, G.P. had been talking of suicide. Not knowing anything about clinical depression, I was no help, yet I felt an urgency to do something, anything to provide some lifeline.

"Since this is our last time together, would you shake my hand and promise that you won't take your life until you phone me first?" I was as shocked as he was by this awkward request. He agreed, shook hands, and was off.

Time passed, and I lost touch with G.P. Several decades later while skiing in Vail, on a particularly frigid morning my wiser ski partners chose to pass on the icy slopes. Arriving alone, bundled up from head to toe, I hopped on a chairlift. My seatmate on the gondola and I made small talk, diverting attention from the frigid conditions. Then he paused and enthusiastically said, "Doug, is that you? This is G.P. I'm still alive." I was stunned.

We talked of years past. Life had been challenging for G.P.; yet it had righted itself. He told me that the act of that simple handshake and vow kept him alive. I was shocked that a seemingly inconsequential and desperate gesture had had such impact.

Then I realized that G.P. was not helped by my genius. All I did was create a safe place for him to be vulnerable; I listened and offered an awkward handshake. Sometimes if we extend ourselves, believe in someone during those dark times, even if we are clueless about how it will work out, we can make a difference. That is what I hope this book will be for you. I believe you have the opportunity to ask the hard questions of yourself and do what is needed to find real purpose.

Know Your Story

> I now see how owning our story and loving
> ourselves through that process is the
> bravest thing that we will ever do.
> —BRENÉ BROWN, RESEARCH PROFESSOR AND AUTHOR

Our story is the central show in living a life of meaning and consequences. Not understanding the various dynamics that have shaped your unique narrative puts you at risk to live someone else's story rather than your own.

Peter Buffett never asked to be the son of one of the wealthiest men on the globe. And yet he had little choice in the matter. His father is multibillionaire Warren Buffett, so doors have easily opened for Peter. If you ask Peter, even his ready entry into Stanford was due to his fabled last name rather than merit. For us lesser mortals, this might not seem like a bad gig, but there is a heavy burden inherent in such an arrangement. Peter's offhand remark to me one day hit me powerfully: "We are all born into someone else's story."

Peter was well aware of that. Because of his status, people expected big things of him. He was on a preset glide path. Then, one day, his personal world abruptly changed. Peter was a sophomore at Stanford when his father famously announced that he wasn't leaving his fortune to his three children. Peter was no longer heir to his father's billions.

His reaction was mixed, understandably so. This was a time to reevaluate. He felt unsettled. Shortly afterward, Peter received news from his mother that his grandfather had left him an inheritance valued at just over $90,000. Clarity came to Peter in an instant. Rather than living his father's story, he would shape his very own.

He dropped out of Stanford, packed his belongings, and drove to New York to launch a music career. He figured he could survive on the amount he had been given for about two years if he watched his spending carefully. He has since become an accomplished musician and songwriter, recognized with a Grammy for his work on the film score of the Kevin Costner blockbuster *Dances with Wolves*. Peter realized that he was not bound to follow only the preset path of Warren Buffett. Peter found his own voice and embraced his unique track when he made that brave decision to leave Stanford and head east. Today, the elder Buffett celebrates his son's personal success, even though it is quite different from his own.

Have you embraced your unique life story apart from the life stories of those who formed you?

We have all been profoundly shaped by the messaging of

our culture as well as our early childhood influences concerning our notions of success, failure, gender roles, and various other life topics. We embrace most of these values and life patterns with little conscious thought or pushback. Although some of this imprinting is surely good, much of it is the source of pain later in life. Often it takes a crisis or an epiphany, as in the cases of Persson and Leonsis, to prompt profound behavioral and attitudinal change. Change is hard.

San Francisco artist and author Elle Luna puts the challenge succinctly. You must understand the difference between *should* and *must*. *Should* is all about societal and parental messaging and expectations, while *must* concerns your personal passion and heart. In her book *The Crossroads of Should and Must*, Luna says, "*Must* is why we are here to begin with, and choosing it is the journey of our lives."[1] Our *shoulds* are absorbed from our surroundings, the messages we get from family and culture. Peter Buffett's *shoulds* caused him to be an unhappy finance major at Stanford; his *must* led him to New York and his music career.

You might not realize how much your background narrative shapes how you live your life, your likes and dislikes, and even your hopes and dreams. Why do I whistle after taking a shower? I heard my mother do this my entire life. Why am I a serial collector? I lived with parents who loved art and antiques. When I was ten, I began assembling an antique wineglass collection.

Rob Kaplan observes, "Each person on this planet has a

life story that is unique. Your story has a powerful impact on your emotions, perceptions, idiosyncrasies, assumptions, vulnerabilities, and mindset. Your story goes a long way toward explaining your behaviors."[2]

Your story doesn't just shape your habits, values, likes, and dislikes; it resonates on a far deeper level. If you're constantly angry, impatient, and prone to rage, there's a strong probability that you observed such behavior growing up. If you're not a forgiver and possess a distrustful nature, you likely experienced that early on as well. Be curious about such things. Although these patterns are often unhelpful and even destructive, they are familiar and hence hold sway over our attitudes and actions. But it does not mean that we are stuck unable to make different decisions and fashion a different life.

With brutal honesty we can begin the process of allowing in the fresh air of new choices. We may feel disloyal to parents when we dare to shift the narrative even slightly, but this is a necessary step in finding our unique path. This could mean letting go of assumptions and false narratives and, frankly, the hopes and expectations of devoted parents and caregivers. By the way, this issue is no respecter of age. The emotions can be raw at whatever point in life these matters are addressed. Make no mistake, this is intense and painful work to undertake. We'd often rather cling to the familiar, despite its poisonous effects, to avoid the risk of blowing up the family story.

Most of us would choose the familiar, finding it too painful to risk change. But equally, we do have the power of choice. As Austrian psychologist Viktor Frankl famously observed in his book *Man's Search for Meaning* (1946), in the death camps of his Nazi captors his fellow prisoners could not control what was done to them, but they could control their attitude toward it. They still had choices available to them, and with choices came the freedom to discover meaning.

The Power of Stories

Several years ago, I attended an event where a simple yet probing question was posed: "What would surprise us to know about you?" Rajiv Kapur, an entrepreneur from Orlando, was seated at my table. When his turn came, Rajiv told us straight-faced that as a child he held the long-distance swimming record in India—for individuals under two years of age! Many of us were skeptical. Could this be true?

Two weeks later, Rajiv sent me an email with an image attached. It was the cover of *Sports Illustrated, India.* It captured a joyous moment: an Olympic diver (Rajiv's father) with his two-year-old son perched for all to see, waving to the adoring crowd. His son, Rajiv, had just won the long-distance swimming record for his age group in India.

Rajiv didn't go on to become a professional swimmer, but that triumph was something he carried with him. It determined his career trajectory—he became a professional tennis player in India and then later in the United States.

Was he conscious of hidden drivers that sparked his career choice? I doubt it. Stories are maps that help us understand others.

Stories are everywhere. Last year, I saw a stirring commercial that demonstrated a simple truth: all around us important, complex, and varied stories are unfolding. The ad had no voiceover, only text that appeared as the camera panned a fast-food restaurant, settling briefly on different individuals and families. Under one woman's image, the text read: "Husband died last Wednesday. Today would have been their fiftieth anniversary." Under another: "Son just deployed to Iraq for the third time." Beside the image of a small girl: "Mother died in childbirth. Father blames child for his wife's death." A glowing girl at the cash register had the tagline: "Thrilled. Just accepted to her dream school."

Unbeknownst to each other, all in that small space comprised an entire ecosystem of brave individuals attempting to make sense of their unique realities, both the good and the challenging. How liberating it would be if we could share candidly with each other, revealing those raw stories and questions. How differently we'd view each other.

Stories are maps that help us locate our pain as well as the source of our strength. They help us understand our behaviors that often seem confusing and unproductive. They offer context. I wondered why an NBA legend never returned to his alma mater even once during the fifty years that followed losing the national championship game. Could it be that the father's dismay with the son's loss on that big collegiate stage haunts the son still?

Once I was traveling with a man I didn't very much care for. I loved his family. He had three children. His middle son was a champion hockey player who ended up playing in the NHL. But this man always struck me as rigid, harsh, and extremely judgmental. One morning, I ran into him in a diner. I'd traveled to see his son's all-star hockey game, and I was hoping to avoid this deeply unpleasant judgmental man. I dreaded the possibility of sharing a meal with him, but had little choice but to invite myself to join him at his table.

As we began to eat, I decided to make the most of the time and probe a bit. I asked him about his personal story. He told me he'd grown up in a small town in Canada, part of a picture-perfect, seemingly normal family of five. Then, in his late thirties, this man discovered a secret truth: his father had two families in that tiny town. His dad had "legally" married two women, had children with both, and had somehow managed to live two distinct lives in that same town.

My breakfast partner explained he had always known something was amiss. He could feel it, and yet could never quite put his finger on the issue. His childhood had been filled with ambiguity and deep anxiety. I pressed to find out how this revelation shaped his story. He simply said, "Since learning the secret of my father's two lives, I have always sought clarity, blacks and whites, no gray areas whatsoever."

Wow. I got it, and now get him. After this conversation,

I had a newfound compassion for this complex man. Not to ponder the story of others is to misread their behavior and intentions. I urge you to dig deep when you sense a hardness or resistance from someone in your circle. Find out more about the people you tend to avoid. They are likely carrying burdens that might surprise you, causing you to shift from judgment to compassion. Every story makes sense if you understand the underlying truth.

I heard once of a father and his five children on an evening subway ride in Brooklyn. While the father looked out the window with a blank stare, his children were acting out in unruly, fitful ways. It was highly disturbing to the other passengers, who finally got his attention.

"Sir, control these hooligans. Their behavior is abhorrent. You are a terrible father!"

The father took in the moment as if waking from a dream. "Oh, I am truly sorry. We just left the Langone Medical Center, where their mother just died."

Although the situation and facts concerning the unruly children were the same, the new information changed everything, causing a shift in perception.

J. D. Vance, in his bestseller *Hillbilly Elegy*, helped many of us understand why working-class Americans are deeply frustrated and bitter, believing that America does not work for them. Many elites thought wrongly that they understood the circumstances of such desperate folks. After spending time with Vance and his book, I now have a new appreciation for and understanding of those wanting a "disrupter" in the White House. Context and story are everything.

We tend to focus only on a narrow circle, those we are comfortable around, certain family, friends, and co-workers. So try shifting that a bit. Talk to a stranger or wander aimlessly in a strange town. It can be an informative and profound experience, and, frankly, humbling.

My good friend John Dalton, former secretary of the navy, once challenged me to reframe a matter. He pointed to the homeless, observing that they never intended to end up on the streets, yet somehow their stories went off track. He said they will tell us a revealing tale, often tragic at its core, if we listen and suspend our judgment and skepticism. For starters, John urged me to ask the homeless their name and how they arrived here. Although uncomfortable at first, I took his challenge to heart.

Soon after that conversation, I went to visit my sister in Portland, Oregon. On a bright summer morning, I went to Rite Aid a few blocks from her apartment in the arts district, the Pearl. As I approached the store, I noticed a large man standing out front asking for money. Most of the passersby ignored him. I gave him some money and then decided to engage. I casually chatted with Randy. We shared our histories.

He had been a seasonal laborer, moving from place to place depending on regional employment opportunities as a farm laborer. Then he severely injured his back. Because he was unable to work and had no health insurance, his only recourse was to beg on the streets. He hated it but had little choice. After learning his story, there was a shift in me. I moved from judgment to compassion. Another thought also struck me: What else am I missing, because I leap to certain conclusions and fail to listen to the heart of another?

Understanding their stories can help you engage with others in a deeper, more authentic way, both personally and professionally. For instance, how can you be a good and enlightened boss if you aren't willing to consider life from your employees' perspective? After all, they have stories too.

CEO Joel Manby was transformed after he took part in the reality television show *Undercover Boss*. As part of the show, Manby worked in disguise as an hourly worker in the very company he ran as chief executive. No one knew his true identity, so people talked to him as a working peer. They told him their stories, some quite tragic, challenging, and raw.

One young man was working full-time at the company while attempting to complete college, also full-time. He was on track to be the first college graduate in his family. He also loved his job and felt that a college degree would help him advance upward. He was living with unimaginable stress, and Manby felt the relentless pressure he struggled under. Another employee, a grounds worker, had lost his home in a flood and was living with his large family crowded into a one-room temporary structure.

From a new vantage point, Manby was able to see the grit

and humanity of the hard-working people scattered through-out his vast enterprise. The effect of learning these highly personal and powerful stories changed Joel. These people with their experiences were always there, hiding in plain sight, but now Joel really saw them up close. He decided to alter the way he ran his company.

It's wonderful when we pivot and let go of our old patterns and habitual ways. The power and wonder of story is everywhere. Just imagine how your approach to leading others would change if you incorporated new eyes of compassion for those in your charge?

Telling Our Own Story

How we choose to interpret our stories and make sense of the inevitable pain and suffering depends on our worldview. The philosopher Friedrich Nietzsche observed that we can endure any *how* as long as we have a *why*. Finding the North Star that grounds us is essential, offering a way to interpret all of life and reality, including the setbacks and blows of life. Such grounding enables us to elevate our thinking and see the redemptive side, even in circumstances of great pain, betrayal, and disappointment.

The first step to uncovering the *why* of your life is to embrace the larger purpose in all you have endured. This will involve both intense introspection and the risk of sharing openly with others. It's a journey of discovery—and storytelling. But candid storytelling has other benefits.

A group of researchers are doing significant work to demonstrate the health benefits of storytelling. As they explain, "Storytelling is emerging as a powerful tool for health promotion in vulnerable populations." They go on to make this compelling conclusion: "Storytelling intervention produced substantial and significant improvements in blood pressure for patients with baseline uncontrolled hypertension."[3] It's no surprise that there are actual physical benefits to being known through story.

Earlier we mentioned former surgeon general Murthy's concern with loneliness as the central health risk of our time. He called loneliness an epidemic throughout society and recommended a simple way to address loneliness in the workplace. Once a week, members of teams should meet to share their stories. They can connect and bond through such storytelling. Co-workers will come together in a different, more human way. Such sharing can even transcend barriers of race, religion, and politics, which often separate us.

We're all facing life issues; let's share openly and benefit from that sense of community connectedness. The atmosphere in the workplace will noticeably change. Co-workers will realize they aren't the only ones struggling. And although the specific issues might vary, most stories contain painful aspects, and that pain can be an avenue for empathy. Authentic sharing enables true community, usually based on our weaknesses rather than our strengths.

So where might we go to understand more deeply the importance of our underlying narrative? Professional resources are available, from psychotherapists to workshops to more intensive programs. Based in the Napa Valley, the Hoffman Process is one such intensive program. It typically requires many hours of prep time answering questions about your family life and early influences before you arrive for the intense nine-day program, but the result is a life-changing time of reflection, bringing new insights and helping you become more healthy and productive.

Whether we avail ourselves of professional help, the point is to commit to understanding our earliest influences, so we can discover our own story, what really drives us and motivates us. To begin, I suggest simply writing out your story in detail and then sharing the unvarnished version with a trusted friend. Don't merely skim the surface. Examine your past, and consider how it impacts your actions today. What did your parents wish for you? What were your earliest dreams of what you would become? What activities have you enjoyed doing the most throughout your life? What were the hardest choices you have had to make, and why did you make them? What has provided the happiest moments in your life? What has caused your most challenging moments?

If you choose not to probe and understand your past, then you are much more likely to repeat the pathologies and behavioral patterns that you were exposed to from your youth. Many of those patterns were highly dysfunctional and destructive. Yet if you honestly consider the truth of that history, it is possible to break free and forge a new and liberating path.

By sharing your story with a friend, you make yourself vulnerable and open to a deeper level of friendship. Your friend's feedback can help you refine your story and see what you might have missed. Whether we work with a friend or a professional therapist, we all could benefit from a better understanding of where we came from and how the story we are born into shaped our present path. Such soul searching, although painful, holds the promise of a liberating outcome.

I tried a variation on this approach recently at a gathering in the Adirondacks hosted by Craig and Connie Weatherup with twenty CEOs and business owners. One of the exercises we did was writing a poem. The mere suggestion of putting pen to paper for this exercise was met with great discomfort and some pushback. But I gave them some help and provided the first three words, "I am from . . ." What resulted was truly extraordinary. The poems were personal and moving, full of self-disclosure and insights. We went from being separate, guarded leaders to a band of real, bonded friends.

The Drive to Please

At the very heart of our stories is the audience we play to, the person or persons we set out to please, consciously or not. This audience is likely a parent or caregiver, a coach, an esteemed teacher, or someone who pushed you to be more than you thought you could be. It is a positive thing to have a champion in the stands, cheering you on. Yet sadly, for many, there is a darker side to this: our audience could be a person—living or dead—who could never be pleased. Or our audience could be an individual who harmed us in some significant way, physically or emotionally. If we do not become aware of who we are unconsciously performing for, we could strive and strive and never secure the deeply needed approval and love we crave. As a result, we could spend a lifetime searching for affirmations and answers in all the wrong places.

A young man came to my office several years ago, seeking my counsel. He was pursuing a career in business. He spoke with such passion about free-market capitalism and entrepreneurship that I inquired, "What's the problem? You seem like you are on a great track. You love what you do, and you're good at it."

He shared that, in his family and culture, being a professional, typically an engineer or medical doctor, was valued above all else. His father, a doctor, wanted him to pursue that same path to achieve social status and security. When the young man chose business, his father stopped speaking to him. He couldn't bear being estranged from this important figure, so he asked what to do.

I paused and explained that he had a choice. He could stay wedded to his father's narrative, or he could take the riskier course in hopes of discovering his own unique passion and purpose. With a tight-knit family, I explained, time was on his side; eventually, God willing, his father would accept his son's professional choices. It isn't easy to diverge from someone whose approval is critically important to you. It is a hard battle, but one worth fighting. If we're brave, we can make our own decisions, decisions that make us our authentic selves. What you say no to is as important, maybe more important, than what you say yes to. As one sage said, "Be yourself. Everyone else is taken."

Our parents aren't the only audience we play to. Peer pressure is frighteningly persuasive as well. We are, at heart, *pleasers*, desperate to do what is expected of us, even if we don't realize it. A recent study of 65,525 financial transactions made during air travel determined that you are 30 percent more likely to make a purchase midair if your seatmate buys something—and this is a stranger, someone you don't consciously care about pleasing![4] We seem almost desperate to secure the approval of others.

A similar phenomenon is "groupthink," which is a pattern of thought in which conformity to group values takes precedence over individual values. The term was originally coined by Irving L. Janis while observing a situation where even more was at stake than air-mall profits and worker intensity. In his book *Groupthink*, Janis writes that although the majority of President Lyndon Johnson's national security team quietly opposed the Vietnam War, they voted in a way that contradicted their personal and often strongly held beliefs. In an official setting, they felt they were expected to support the war effort. Those Cabinet officers bent to the will of the group and their powerful president, though ironically the majority sentiment was the opposite.[5]

"Groupthink" can be frightening and a cause for serious concern when you consider the atrocities committed throughout history. The groupthink dynamic can be insidious because people are not aware it is occurring. How many awful events were the result of decisions made in situations where uniform behavior trumped personal values and beliefs?

It takes a lot of courage to stand up for what you personally believe, particularly when an audience—with a consensus—pushes you to act differently and rewards you accordingly. Social scientists have concluded that it is almost impossible to dissent from expectations that have become the group standard, even if they are wrong or immoral.

In the famous Stanford prison experiment of 1971, twenty-four student subjects were separated into two groups, "guards" and "inmates," in a basement that served as a mock prison. After six days, the experiment had to be abandoned, because it had spiraled dangerously out of control. The "guards" had begun to threaten the safety of the "inmates." Later, one of the most abusive guards reflected that his behavior wasn't the result of being thrust into an evil environment. Instead, he was driven by one objective, to please his prison supervisor. He would have done anything to gain his acceptance. Even though the guards and inmates were role-playing in an artificially created environment, the audiences they catered to felt quite real to them, compelling the guards to act in surprising ways.

And no matter how powerful or evolved as a person you are, these pressures remain and are real. I realized this as a young White House staffer in a private Oval Office meeting with President Reagan and his top three aides, James Baker, Edwin Meese, and Michael Deaver. I was a lowly notetaker in this meeting. The discussion focused upon Reagan's likely Democratic opponent for a second term, Senator Ted Kennedy. At least three times, his closest aides remarked that the president was far superior to his morally bankrupt opponent. And shockingly, each time the president stopped their critique, choosing not to join in, and simply said, "The Kennedys, they have suffered so much."

The scene was remarkable for its demonstration of resistance to peer pressure and "groupthink." When your friends are affirming you and lavishing praise upon you, it takes real guts to take a quiet stand in opposition. I returned to my office, recalling what an inspired display of character I had just witnessed. Here was the leader of the free world, marching to his own beat and standing against even close friends. Rare in public life.

In his book *The Lonely Crowd*, David Riesman studies the manner in which a society ensures a certain degree of conformity from its members. Children learn various modes of conformity from an early age, Riesman explains. He identifies several categories of conformity, "tradition-directed," "inner-directed," and "other-directed," but the one that stands out for me is the last. This is the child who is constantly under pressure from parents, particularly, to rise to high status among his or her peers. Riesman explains: "The peer-group becomes much more important to the child, while the parents make him feel guilty not so much about violation of inner standards as about failure to be popular." This child is taught both at home and in society that popularity is more important than authenticity or even integrity. For "other-directed" people, Riesman notes, "contemporaries are the source of direction."[6]

How's that for a fickle "audience"? *The Lonely Crowd* was originally published in 1950, but in today's world, with pressures to conform even more pronounced than in previous times, its findings are even more alarming.

Whom do you strive to please? What or who is driving your behavior and habits, your values, your ambitions and notions of success? If you understand who or what is propelling you in some direction, you might choose to rethink and course-correct.

Who Is the Audience?

In the next chapter we will discuss the importance of maintaining a close-knit community of friends who can serve as a core audience to help us live up to our deepest values and purposes for our lives. But here I want to discuss the other groups that influence us, often in ways that distance us from these goals.

Is it possible to live a genuine life true to ourselves without being pressured to conform to the audiences around us? It's important to remember that, even as an individual, you have choices. You can resist expectations, rather than acquiesce. Riesman describes this type of independence as "inner direction." The "inner-directed" person possesses an internal gyroscope that enables a steady course despite the prevailing winds of popular sentiment.

I have often fallen short of being an "inner-directed" person—but not in all cases. During my second semester in college at the University of North Carolina, Chapel Hill, I reached a crisis point. I had pledged to join a fraternity, yet was never fully comfortable with the implicit demands of the brotherhood. I wasn't interested in a regimen of binge drinking and carousing. Since I was an athlete, the fraternity cut me some slack.

Then one particular evening, Hell Night, the brothers of the house decided to publicly shred what they thought was my goody-goody facade. It was late, around three o'clock in the morning. We were all in the great room of the Tudor-style ATO House on Franklin Street. The twenty pledges were paraded before the brotherhood, awaiting their individual moment of humiliation and verbal abuse. They saved me till last. The brothers were pushing me to get drunk and do several other things I resisted. I'd never before been put in a situation of such intense group pressure and expectation. From the back of the room, an older fraternity brother and dear friend to this day, John Yates, caught my eye. He looked equally at sea as to what I should do.

Then, in a moment of defiant lucidity, I blurted out, "If I have to change fundamentally who I am, I resign as a pledge." Then I abruptly left the room. John met me outside, where I immediately broke down in tears of humiliation.

We walked back to my dorm room in Alexander Hall. At that point, I considered transferring schools or joining the witness-protection program. I was utterly ashamed and humiliated. It was a true low point. I think of what that wise sage Homer Simpson once mused, "This is not the worst day of your life, only the worst day so far." This was certainly the worst day so far!

Then something remarkable happened. An hour or so later, there was a knock on my dorm-room door. Standing there was the fraternity president. He asked me to come outside. The entire fraternity had assembled in front of my dorm. There was an eerie silence. They then apologized.

I felt awkward, yet somehow deeply reassured. It was a significant moment, the first time I took a stand that cost me something—and I was ultimately respected for it. I'm no hero, just one suck-up who occasionally gets it right. The earlier in life you become comfortable with standing alone, the greater the freedom you will experience from the unhealthy expectations of others. It's a continual struggle to resist the urge merely to please.

Soon after President Trump was elected, thirty members of Congress asked me to join them to discuss a hero of mine, the British abolitionist William Wilberforce. He was a highly principled leader who labored for forty-five years to abolish slavery in the British Empire. Wilberforce was ultimately successful, and yet it cost him dearly; his health, wealth, and reputation all suffered. Additionally, he gave up various opportunities for political advancement and influence, choosing to pursue a path of contribution over that of self-service.

Although the composition of the group I was speaking to was mostly Republican, there were several Democrats on hand as well. Following my remarks, they surprised me with a question: "What do you think of us as congressional leaders?"

I asked if they wanted my candid observations.

They did.

I obliged by saying that I thought individually they were high-minded and principled, but as a legislative body they were a disaster and an embarrassment. My answer shocked a bit.

They then asked what I would propose they do. I told them that in my view the context was the problem. For a variety of reasons, there is no ability to cooperate across party lines to get anything done, since the culture of the legislative body has become so dysfunctional and mean-spirited, with the extremes fueled by unlimited money and cable television. I then paused and said simply, "Do the right thing!"

I went on: "If you are a Republican, find an issue that matters and work across the aisle to get it accomplished. And if you get voted out, so be it. Would you rather tell your grandchildren you occupied a seat in Congress or you lost doing something that mattered for the greater good of the nation? It might be costly, and you might even get fired. But learn from the example of former attorney general Elliot Richardson, who served under Richard Nixon. When pressured to fire special counsel Archibald Cox, who was investigating Watergate crimes, Richardson refused and resigned in protest. How glorious was that? He clearly had the right audience in mind when he took such a costly stand."

Someone who seems to have found his voice and audience is former South Carolina governor and congressman Mark Sanford. You will recall that Mark had a very public failing in 2009: he falsely claimed to be hiking the Appalachian Trail, when he was actually with his Argentine mistress in South America. After learning of my friend's challenging ordeal, Steve Case, Bob Woody, and I flew to South Carolina to be with him, to simply listen and offer perspective.

Over the ensuing months and years, I have seen Mark evolve from a "pleaser" to a principled leader who is challenging his own party and president with little hesitation. Having survived the crucible of his public failure, Mark now sees himself as a "dead man walking." As he says, "If you've already been dead, you don't fear it as much. I've been dead politically." And although he is the most unlikely enforcer of honesty in politics, he is playing a unique role as the nation's conscience, all resulting from discovering a new audience.

The best leaders, in my opinion, are people who seek to accomplish something, even when it is unpopular and hard, because it is the right thing to do. I asked Jonathan Aitken, former member of the British Parliament, what was different about parliamentarians in the Thatcher era, how they compared with those of the present day. He told me with no hesitation that in the Thatcher era, when he served, certain members of Parliament had been through the experience of World War II. Following the war years, these politicians were not intimidated by criticism or threatening rhetoric of any sort. It's not easy to bully World War II vets who took down Nazi aircraft and fought to save our very civilization. Today, we are electing mere "pleasers," those who have not been tested deep within, he explained. They so desperately long to be liked and reelected that they often forget why they ran in the first place.

In his book *Originals*, Adam Grant carefully examines the effectiveness of leaders. He reviewed evaluations of American presidents from a myriad of historians, psychologists, and political scientists. He wanted to understand which presidents were successful and why. The data determined that the least effective leaders were ones who followed the will of the people and the precedents of former commanders in chief. The "great" presidents challenged the status quo and brought sweeping change to the nation, despite harsh criticism, which was often quite personal and mean-spirited. The most effective leaders marched to their own beat. It's no surprise that Abraham Lincoln scored highest, because he did what needed to be done, though it was costly.[7]

Some years ago an Australian nurse, Bronnie Ware, pinpointed the most common regrets of the dying in a nursing home where she worked. It was phrased in a variety of ways, but the sentiment was surprisingly consistent: they all regretted a lack of courage to have lived a life true to themselves, rather than what was expected of them.[8] Isn't that a pattern we're all familiar with? We all seem to have voices real or imagined that we spend a lifetime seeking to please. Why do we empower others to determine our happiness or define success for us? In my view, this almost insatiable need to please everyone is at the root of so much of our unhappiness, both personally and professionally.

In a 2014 *New York Times* documentary titled *Slomo*, I was introduced to a most unusual former North Carolina neurologist who traded his lucrative medical practice for a bohemian existence of freedom and self-expression. Dr. John Kitchin, now self-identified as Slomo, spends his days rollerblading along the boardwalk of San Diego's Pacific Beach. What got him to this place was an epiphany one afternoon while chatting with an elderly man in his hospital cafeteria. The elderly man told Kitchin his secret to happiness: "Do what you want!"

It hit the eminent neurologist like a lightning bolt. He suddenly realized that he had spent his entire life living up to others' expectations. He had created a life with all the

markings of success—the mansion, the exotic bird collection, the Ferrari. His prime goal had been the admiration of
peers. But now freedom and true peace meant living simply
and rollerblading every day, period. Slomo had found a new
audience—himself.

No doubt a healthy debate could be had about the merits
of a life in the pursuit of pleasure rather than one of service.
After all, Kitchin had medical gifts desperately needed by
suffering patients. I certainly understand that line of reason-
ing. But as he says, "I was one who escaped from the grip of
convention and expectation." So, as in most stories, the truth
is messy and complicated, but his story has a point, and one
worthy of consideration and discussion.

Become Your Own Audience

One way to develop a deeper understanding of your story
is to become your own audience. Take yourself out of your
story and tell it. Are you inspired by the person at the helm
in that narrative? Do you feel that this person is engaging
with others authentically? Is this person motivated by personal beliefs or others' definitions of success? Is this person
desperate to appear strong, even when feeling powerless?
Do you admire him or her?

Years ago, my close friend Steve Case, cofounder of AOL,
and I flew down to Asheville, North Carolina, for a private

visit with Billy Graham. Graham's health had been failing, and Steve wanted to spend as much time with this remarkable figure and close friend as possible. Graham's influence in the world was beyond measure. He had spoken to more people than anyone in history!

We arrived and found Graham fragile, relying heavily on a walker. Although he was obviously quite frail, I was impressed by his endurance and lucidity. We spoke for hours. Steve graciously allowed me to ask question after question, ranging from Graham's relationship with JFK and the Mormon hotel magnate Willard Marriott to his view of Muslims and their spiritual destiny. Graham's humility and lack of rigidity and judgment were striking. His thinking had clearly evolved. He patiently and with utter candor answered all inquiries until a certain moment abruptly altered the rhythm of our exchange. He took a bead on me with those steel-blue penetrating eyes.

"Doug, you have asked me questions all day. Could I ask you one? I need your advice." I gulped and nodded, panic gripping my face.

"As you can see, I am much diminished. I use a walker and am extremely weary and spent. I am in my eighties but am getting calls from news networks around the world to be interviewed about my life and the state of the world." Then came the showstopper. "Do you think that the public should see me in my weakened state, or should they remember me as the firebrand of old?"

I paused and pondered what I could possibly offer this

giant figure. But then I had a thought. "If Pope John Paul II has taught us anything, it has been the power of his genuine humanity in the face of decline. Despite a serious stroke that left him partially paralyzed, the pope travels and shows that his weakness and infirmity are not a limitation, but are inevitable as we age and decline. Weakness need not be feared and despised, even in a culture that prizes and elevates youth and beauty." I urged Graham to allow the world to experience him in decline. This too would be inspirational, perhaps even more so than his earlier labors.

Graham was humble, asking for guidance mainly because he so desperately desired to finish well and to please the right audience.

Most of us want to present a story to others that highlights only the achievements and wins. Yet far more interesting and valuable are those failures and low points where we started paying attention to what matters. Everyone can identify with brokenness and setback; after all, it is reality, if you live long enough.

Dale Jones was asked to take the helm of a global executive-search firm based in Philadelphia. Dale shared with me this piece of advice he was given at the start of his tenure: "When you are interviewing CEO candidates for new job opportunities, ask them about the 'failed rungs' on their ladder. If they can't tell you some, run for the hills." Everyone, if they are honest, has experienced setback and limitations. Real leaders don't run from weakness; they embrace and incorporate it into their authentic leadership style.

No doubt exposing our limitations and failures is risky. We are taught from day one to project strength, to be unflappable. So much that occurs in our lives shapes our stories in unexpected ways and can easily derail us through discouragement and setback. Yet the questing for purpose is all about becoming whole, embracing all facets of who we are.

Author Richard Rohr understands the difference between circumstances and our real lives: "Most people confuse their life situation with their actual life, which is an underlying flow beneath the everyday events."[9]

It's important to consider who you are, the real story that drives you, not the fake one you learn to project. You aren't simply the sum of your achievements and failures. You aren't defined by the status associated with powerful individuals you just met, the job you just lost, or the raise you just received. You are a complex being who has been influenced by people and circumstances that existed long before you did and those that will exist long after you pass.

It is both illuminating and chilling to understand this map in its entirety. Yet once you fully accept your truth, truly embrace it, you will then have choices. You can live the story of your peers and family or you can value your own story and find your own path. For in the end, to be healthy and the best version of yourself, there must be separation. You and I must differentiate ourselves from our past, letting go of the patterns that continually sabotage our lives in the present. Listen to the audience that truly matters: the audience of one.

In my case, faith in an ever-present God is my core audience, at least aspirationally. I find meaning in that arrangement. Jean-Paul Sartre spoke for me when he stated: "No finite point has meaning without an infinite reference point." But we all must determine our audience and reference point. It requires courage to be truly you. As the American poet Ralph Waldo Emerson rightly observed: "To be yourself in a world that is constantly trying to make you something else is the greatest accomplishment." Be brave.

We all have an audience, perhaps multiple. And we all have a story. It is vital to reflect upon our initial questions if we are to move forward living the story true to ourselves. "Have you embraced your unique life story and identified your audience?" It is a critically important question to consider, for it is the doorway to a life of meaning.

TAKE ACTION:
Learning Your Own Story

We are all born into someone else's story.
—PETER BUFFETT, SON OF FINANCIER WARREN BUFFETT

In your journal reflect on these questions and exercises:

• *Write out your story in at least three pages as it comes to your mind; include the good, the bad, and the ugly.*

Don't overthink this exercise; let the thoughts flow freely.

• *Now read over what you wrote. Are there parts of your story you are ashamed of?*

• *Write out a brief outline of your parents' (or caregivers') stories. If possible, ask each of your parents (or caregivers) about their story and what shaped their own journey. What was their relationship with their parents like? How does it compare with your relationship to your parents?*

• *Did you feel shame or embarrassment about your parents or caregivers when you were growing up? In what way?*

• *Write down ten positive traits of each parent or caregiver. Now record ten negative qualities that you experienced firsthand. Finally, circle those specific traits from both lists that you brought into your story and experience.*

• *Who is your audience and how does this impact how you live your life?*

• *What would you do differently if you weren't afraid of disappointing your audience?*

Maintain Genuine Relationships

If you want to go fast, go alone.

If you want to go far, go together.

—AFRICAN PROVERB

Two are better than one, because they have a good
reward for their labor. For if they fall, one will lift
up his companion. But woe to him who is alone
when he falls, for he has no one to help him up.

—ECCLESIASTES 4:9–10 (NKJV)

O n a cool summer evening in July, I sat on an ancient
wooden ferry chugging along in the Gulf of Nicoya in
Costa Rica. Next to me sat one of my lifelong friends, Juan
Edgar Picado, then a promising young attorney in the capital
city of San José. We were two young men wanting to make a
difference in the world and delighting in one another's company. We spoke candidly and comfortably of our hopes, fears,

and the various challenges awaiting our attention. Our conversation was punctuated with hearty bursts of laughter that at points became almost uncontrollable.

Watching from a nearby bench was a middle-aged Costa Rican gentleman. Curious, the onlooker hesitantly approached, declaring, "I don't know what philosophy or religion you two subscribe to, but whatever it is, I'd like to join."

Unsure whether to celebrate or be concerned, we looked at one another as if to say, "Yep, life is good." We had not realized how powerful a magnet an authentic relationship could be. I suspect this gentleman was drawn by something genuine he observed between two flawed humans who were deeply connecting, something increasingly rare in our impersonal yet technologically connected world.

Without rich long-term relationships, it is simply impossible to live lives of meaning and purpose. That is why friendships are so important. But maintaining genuine relationships long term has become almost countercultural.

A dear friend, David Rogers, CEO of the H. E. Butt Foundation in San Antonio, posed a fascinating hypothetical question to author David Brooks: "What would you do with several million dollars? What does the world need right now?" Brooks's response appeared in his syndicated column in the *New York Times* several weeks later: "Friendship is not in great shape in America today, . . . [so] I'd try to set up places that would cultivate friendships." He continued, "I envision a string of adult camps or retreat centers . . . to spark bonds between disparate individuals."[1]

It seems odd to imagine, yet the simple experience of friendship has fallen on hard times in recent decades. The evidence points to the reality that most of us have fewer and fewer friends as we age. But this wasn't always the case. This most mysterious of all human associations has occupied the minds and pens of many notable poets and thinkers throughout history.

The theme of friendship has shaped plot lines in great texts from Homer to Shakespeare and in the short stories of James Joyce, Anton Chekhov, and Nadine Gordimer. Philosophers and essayists Aristotle and Cicero to Montaigne and Emerson have extolled its virtues. Friendship fired the correspondence of Wolfgang Mozart, John Keats, Gustave Flaubert, Oscar Wilde, T. S. Eliot, Virginia Woolf, and countless others. Reading the poems of William Blake and Walt Whitman and the comic vignettes of Colette, one can see that friendship was central to their worldviews and day-to-day experience.

Our present crisis of societal loneliness has prompted many to search, like the man in Costa Rica, for some deeper association. Some are longing for real, enduring, and honest friendships that address the full scope of our humanity. Small groups are a promising countertrend to the plight of our isolation.

There are countless groups designed to bring both men and women together through a common interest, such as faith-based groups, twelve-step programs, and industry-related gatherings. It's just a matter of intentionally creating space and priority in our hectic schedules and locating the group that is the right fit. Whether you're joining a small group or making an individual connection, the fact remains that we were made for such intimate associations. To have a life of meaning and purpose, maintaining deep relationships is a necessity.

Often quoted in marriage ceremonies, the book of Genesis in the Torah proclaims, "It is not good for the man to be alone."[2] This doesn't just apply to marriage. When we become isolated, bad things happen. We were designed by our Creator to regularly connect with others on an emotional level, a soul level, beyond even words at times. Without genuine relationships, we wither in heart and mind. This is why solitary confinement is so torturous and the ultimate horrific punishment.

As noted, Harvard professor Robert Putnam highlighted the demise of bowling leagues and PTA meetings as a metaphor for our increasingly fractionalized and solitary society. For the first two-thirds of the twentieth century, a powerful tide of social engagement swept the nation. The shift away from civic connection has been dramatic and swift, and loneliness and isolation are now rampant. The change is apparent in the decline of poker and bridge clubs, dwindling church attendance, and reduced interest in other traditional groups. De Tocqueville, who saw civic engagement and interest in various small associations as the primary strength of a young nation, would be shocked.

Lonely at the Top

Success in business or other endeavors can exacerbate the problem. It has become a cliché to say, "It's lonely at the top." Yet the fact remains that success can actually put people at risk to become even more lonely and disconnected, particularly men. In a candid conversation about friendship at the 2017 Obama Foundation Summit, former first lady Michelle Obama said, "Women, we do it better than men.... Y'all should get you some friends. Get you some friends and talk to each other." She added that she wanted her husband, former president Barack Obama, to enlarge his group of male friends. At one point, she said, "Y'all need to go talk to each other about your stuff, because there's so *much* of it. It's so messy."[3]

Indeed, our fear of being really known, warts and all, causes us to hide and be reluctant to engage, since such vulnerability comes at the risk of rejection. Whether you are president or a simple working stiff, you probably firmly believe that if anyone really knew you, you would be neither liked nor accepted. As that great philosopher Groucho Marx once mused, "I don't want to belong to any club that will accept me as a member." So we hide, fearful to be known and reveal the very things that would connect us and create common ground with others.

Research supports the view that leaders, especially CEOs, become isolated. It is almost inherent in the role. Jessica Stillman wrote in a 2012 *Inc.* article about RHR International's survey of eighty-three CEOs of public and private companies with annual revenues of $50 million to $2 billion. They found that fully half of those top executives reported a sense of isolation affecting their ability to function in their jobs.[4]

There are times when who we are is revealed for all to see whether we like it or not. It is not only humiliating, but tests the bonds of friendship. Although some friendships survive such a time, many do not. Two Stanford roommates graduated and created professional lives that by all outward appearances functioned beautifully. Both were wealthy men seemingly at the top of their game. Then the unthinkable happened. James Bottomley chose to murder his mistress.

Any way you tried to understand this, it made no sense. But the story here is not one of murder and life imprisonment, but rather one of friendship. My friend, Jim Jameson, rather than dropping his former roommate, as most would have, embraced him and leaned into their friendship. Obviously, this was a highly unusual counterintuitive response. This has resulted in a decades-long correspondence between the two, captured in the book *Across the Bars*.[5]

Their journey together caused my friend to ponder the nature of unconditional love. Questions arose. Can friendships survive the worst of transgressions? Does redemption exist for a murderer? Can hope be found despite a life sentence? Both Jims discovered a level of friendship and commitment uncommon in our world. By refusing to dissolve their relationship, both men were changed forever, sharing a dimension of love and loyalty few experience. I think of what Augustine mused centuries earlier: "They are my true brothers, because whether they see good in me or evil, they love me still."

Sometimes we are surprised when we are the recipients of grace and love in unexpected ways—something that committed friends are in a position to offer each other. Surely Jim Bottomley had such a moment when his Stanford roommate refused to give up on him.

The longing for human connection and some sense of belonging are often revealed by their absence. When überwealthy hedge-fund manager Joseph "Chip" Skowron III returned to his tony Greenwich, Connecticut, community after serving five years in federal prison for insider trading, surprisingly he experienced a profound sense of emptiness along with severe peer judgment. He reflected, "I really feel most comfortable in prison." Prison for Skowron offered true community, friendship, and lack of judgment. Reflecting upon his privileged life prior to incarceration, he said, "I wanted to be somebody that was important. I wanted to accomplish, succeed, to be satisfied. It was all illusory." Since his release, Skowron returns to prison several times per week to experience authentic relationships and to encourage others still serving time.[6]

When my former boss at the White House, Robert "Bud" McFarlane, the National Security Advisor, went through a dark patch resulting in a failed suicide attempt, he told me a surprising story. He awoke the next day at Sibley Hospital, still reeling from the ordeal, only to find sitting at his bedside former president Richard Nixon. This was well after the former president had resigned in disgrace. You might recall that Nixon struggled with a blood clot in his leg (phlebitis), which prevented him from flying in his later years. Yet Nixon had hopped on the shuttle from New York and appeared at Bud's side, anxiously awaiting his return to consciousness. His only message to Bud was straightforward and from the heart: "I've felt the despair you are feeling. God has a purpose for you still."

Nixon risked his health to deliver that one simple thought. This was certainly a case of someone being a "wounded healer" to a fellow in need. True friendship is not a quid pro quo relationship, but one that goes above and beyond, never counting the cost.

It is powerful and moving when a friend simply shows up devoid of fanfare to offer support and presence. Skip Ryan was such a friend to me when I accepted a demanding post at the Department of State prior to the dramatic release of Nelson Mandela. My task was hard and complex: develop the US response to the challenges posed by apartheid in South Africa. Skip simply showed up one day. He literally put his job and personal agenda aside and offered to help his friend who felt so woefully inadequate for the responsibilities awaiting his attention. Friendship is like that—people who simply show up, like Nixon and my friend Skip, and through their mere presence engender hope and possibility.

Sacrifice was clearly in Minnesota governor Al Quie's mind when he offered to serve the remaining prison sentence for his friend and Watergate felon Chuck Colson. You might recall that Colson was hardly a beloved figure in American politics. He was referred to as "Nixon's hatchet man," an apt description. He once boasted that he would drive over his own grandmother to have Nixon reelected. When Al revealed to me that he had discovered the legal means to substitute himself for Colson, I was aghast. Yes, visit him, pray for him, even lend financial support to his family—but serve his jail sentence? No way. But Al had discovered another dimension of the wonder and mystery of friendship—sacrifice. Surely Colson's sense of isolation was offset by such a friend's remarkable offer.

Isolation can be real for all of us, not just those sentenced to prison or struggling with dark thoughts of suicide. In *The Lonely City: Adventures in the Art of Being Alone*, Olivia Laing describes well the true nature of loneliness:

> Loneliness is hallmarked by an intense desire to bring the experience to a close; something which cannot be achieved by sheer willpower or by simply getting out more, but only by developing intimate connections. This is far easier said than done, especially for people whose loneliness arises from a state of loss or exile or prejudice, who have reason to fear or mistrust as well as long for the society of others.[7]

With screens surrounding our every move, true human communication can be ever more precious and rare. This is why a handwritten note makes such a marked impression in our digital age. In the early 1970s, Alvin Toffler wrote *Future Shock*, and Vance Packard, *A Nation of Strangers*, and still no one could have anticipated the unprecedented affluence and myriad technologies of convenience that today separate us further. Young people are redefining what friendship is, meeting friends through their devices, and often continuing that friendship exclusively online. Is this simply a new manifestation or expression of friendship in the digital age? Should we be concerned?

The director of a Harvard medical clinic devoted exclusively to the maladies of children caused by technology told me two jarring facts. First, one-third of young people have a "best" friend whom they have never physically met, and second, the most common problem he treats is sleep deprivation; since children don't turn off their devices at night, they are constantly awakened by the buzzing and noise and fail to enter into deep REM sleep patterns. It stems, it seems, from that most modern of obsessions, FOMO—fear of missing out!

When telephones were introduced in the late nineteenth century, people were afraid that families would be destroyed by such intrusion into home life. Each age fears the abuses of technology. It's important to discuss what we potentially lose with the advent of each new advance in technology and also what we potentially gain. There are certainly more opportunities to connect globally. What kinds of conversations are you striking up with individuals online? What about offline?

Are you seeking out genuine relationships? Are you lonely, despite a myriad of friends and "likes" online? Perhaps these are the questions we should be considering.

The Harvard Grant Study is the longest longitudinal study ever undertaken, tracking 268 Harvard men for seventy-five years. The study has some limitations, since it didn't include women when the project was launched in 1939. Yet it does provide an unrivaled peek into a subset of humanity by collecting data annually on various aspects of the lives and values of this group as they age. This study is less a theoretical piece of work than a practical investigation into the things that make for a happy and purposeful life.

George Vaillant, the Harvard psychiatrist who directed a portion of this important study from 1972 to 2004, pointed out that, by far, the most important finding is that relationships, period, are what matter in life. Vaillant observed that a man could have a successful career, money, and good physical health, but without supportive, loving relationships would not be happy.[8] This is a powerful research-based analysis that concludes the obvious.

But the question remains: So why do we tend to chase after every shiny thing *but* relationships to fill that human void?

Perhaps the voice of experience might offer a clue. Atlanta author and friend Steve Franklin and a colleague conducted a fascinating research project in which they interviewed over five hundred centenarians (people over one hundred years old) about their secrets and wisdom for having a happy, fulfilling life. Mentioned most frequently were *gratitude, faith*, and *staying connected to others*.[9]

Loneliness doesn't hurt just on an emotional level. Research has highlighted that loneliness affects the health of older adults as much as obesity. John Cacioppo, professor of psychology at the University of Chicago, observes in *Loneliness: Human Nature and the Need for Social Connection* that there is evidence loneliness affects mental and physical well-being and chronic loneliness belongs among health factors such as smoking, obesity, and lack of exercise.[10] Loneliness is a truly destructive state.

Sadly, loneliness can even lead to suicide. Bestselling author Gail Sheehy, in *Understanding Men's Passages*, interviewed hundreds of men about various aspects of their lives. She discovered in her research that the average age of men who committed suicide was sixty-three.[11] Why? At that age, you have perhaps retired, maybe not having achieved what you had hoped. Or perhaps you sold your private company. You find yourself stuck in a pointless job with no prospects for retirement. Either way, you have been working hard, nonstop, for decades, typically defining your identity and sense of self-worth through work alone. A crisis awaits when this artificial prop is suddenly removed, signaling a new unsettling and lonely chapter in your life.

Thomas Merton observed that we tend to be "doers" rather than "*be*-ers." In *No Man Is an Island*, Merton notes, "The less he is able to *be* the more he has to *do*."[12] When the job is removed, there is often a huge void. In my experience, most men, unlike women, find such terrain later in life extremely difficult to understand and navigate. Many men simply don't have the requisite tools to do so, including a language to discuss what they feel. Often men are raised to be strong and self-reliant. How's that working?

But this existential feeling of dread and isolation isn't exclusive to any economic status or gender. Anyone who chases one accomplishment after the next, without consistent time for reflection and the nurture of relationships, will ultimately be left with every*thing*, but too frequently no one to be with.

The importance of relationships doesn't apply only to retirement or the end game. One mustn't underestimate the power of having friends along the way while you are building a career. Whether you are just starting out or are decades into a high-pressured career, friends can keep you grounded during various seasons. They can offer insights as you ponder a bold move. They can remind you that it's a big world and help keep things in perspective. They can show you that you're not alone and that we all have similar moments, those times you feel trapped or fearful and need reassurance. They can even call you out when you start to think too highly of yourself and thus forget your deeper priorities, vulnerable moments when we are all prone to make bad choices.

Simple friendship can seem a luxury for busy, success-obsessed people, but it should be a core value for anyone in search of greater meaning. We are created for relationship.

It is oxygen for the soul. We must simply build it into our busy routines, time for those important to us. I'm not talking about superficial buddies. For a friendship to have true value, it must be genuine and deep, with an element of risk and vulnerability.

Beyond Networking

I loathe the term *networking*. It reduces the richness of human association to a mere commodity, a thing to help you advance your professional ambitions. There's much more to peers and elders than seeing them as useful for your pragmatic purposes. On the other hand, if you forge true connections with people in your industry, relationships of trust, you'll find that they often help you accomplish great things and overcome daunting obstacles. But that should be a by-product rather than the motivation for establishing them.

Mutual benefit is the essence of true friendship, making both parties better through the association. Consider the long friendship between Thomas Jefferson and James Madison. Together, they helped establish the character of America. Samuel Coleridge and William Wordsworth inspired one another to write poetry that neither would have produced alone. The intellectual and spiritual friendship of C. S. Lewis and J. R. R. Tolkien is justly celebrated for shaping their important writings, which have sold in the millions.

Warren Buffett and Charlie Munger, business partners for decades, relish their odd relationship. Buffett loves Munger's curiosity and breadth of knowledge, which he cites as bringing invaluable perspective to both their investments and his life.

We're programmed to think that we need friends for advancement. How sad. How about once you've reached those lofty ambitions? What then? A group of well-known CEOs formed a support circle for one another soon after they were each named to head giant global companies. Members included Steve Reinemund, chair and CEO of PepsiCo; Jeff Immelt, chair and CEO of GE; Bill Weldon, chair and CEO of Johnson & Johnson; and a few others. Their aim, rather than to generate business, was to foster a peer-to-peer time of deep sharing and friendship. They wanted to gain perspective by connecting with those in similar positions yet different industries.

They all understood that their public profiles, by definition, tended to isolate. They were all in search of "truth tellers" who had their best interests at heart. They all dealt regularly with the same unrelenting pressure from Wall Street as well as shareholders, not to mention the media. Few not in their position understood the unique challenges each faced at that rarefied level. Peers can serve as fresh eyes, providing objective perspective in our efforts to winnow out the urgent from the important.

The book of Proverbs says: "As iron sharpens iron, so a

man sharpens the countenance of his friend."[13] Bill Weldon, of Johnson & Johnson, told me that when the Tylenol scandal broke, something potentially devastating for his company, one CEO in this group drove to New Brunswick and just sat with him in his office. Sometimes the mere presence of a trusted friend is as powerful as any advice.

It's important to forge trusted relationships, and not always with people you naturally gravitate toward. It can be life-altering to connect with someone whose background and life experience are different from your own. I've personally benefitted by serving on the board of Morehouse College, a historically black all-male institution in Atlanta, where I am a minority. It has been both inspirational and enlightening to share time and friendship with the extraordinary leaders on the board. They view life differently, and it has enriched my life and broadened me as a leader.

The reality of engaging someone truly dissimilar to oneself came sharply into focus for Daryl Davis one night in 1983. He and his country band were performing at a truckstop lounge. During a break, Davis, an African American, was approached by a white man who admired his "Jerry Lee Lewis–like" piano playing. He offered to buy Davis a drink. Then, while they sat together, this man told Davis he'd never previously had a drink with a black man. He went on to explain that he was a card-carrying member of the Ku Klux Klan.

Davis burst out laughing until the man slid his Klan

membership card in front of him. Davis wondered, "How could anybody hate me when they don't even know me?"

He decided to explore this question by getting to know the man who had just told him about his deep hostility toward black people. In the process, this Klan member, Frank James, would have his world turned upside down. By getting to know Davis firsthand, James's entire outlook shifted. He realized how wrong it was to cling to such racist, bigoted views. Yet the pathway to this enlightened perspective had been a relationship, not information. He eventually resigned from the Klan.

Yet Davis didn't stop with one man. He decided to travel the country and interview Klan members from various chapters, always with that haunting question in his mind, "Why do they hate me when they don't know me?"

Davis became friends with many Klan members, including Roger Kelly, the Imperial Wizard, the top national leader of the Klan. After being in the Klan for over twenty years, Kelly resigned from the KKK because of his friendship with Davis. He apologized to Davis and gave him his robe and hood to symbolize his change of heart. He is now one of Davis's best friends.[14] It is hard to vilify someone you know personally. Our humanity connects us. Most of our fears of the "other" disappear when we truly know others personally, when we know their stories, their hopes and fears.

To state the obvious, divisions and mistrust in our nation are at an all-time high. Under the inspiration and chiding of Secretary John Dalton, several of us recently launched a civility luncheon series to showcase unlikely partnerships, people who found a way to see each other as real humans despite deep differences. We wanted to expose individuals of influence to actual models of civility, hoping that perhaps it would inspire them to think and act differently.

Two individuals from vastly different backgrounds and worldviews recently joined us for an animated session: Imam Mohamed Magid and Pastor Bob Roberts Jr. Magid is a Sudanese Muslim cleric, leader of the All Dulles Area Muslim Society (ADAMS) and former president of the Islamic Society of North America (ISNA). He has been a key adviser to presidents Obama and Bush as well as a trusted confidant of the FBI. Roberts pastors a large evangelical church in Fort Worth, Texas. By his own admission, Roberts is an ardent conservative and card-carrying member of the NRA. These two men have chosen to engage one another and overcome the natural biases of their respective faith communities. They have spoken at each other's gatherings, traveled the world together, and have urged others in their communities to follow their example. They urge their congregants to reject fear and bias and to get to know each other as people and as families.

As these men have demonstrated, once trust is established, it's possible to start talking about and tackling the difficult sensitive matters that divide. It's critical to explore our inherent prejudices—we all have them. Do you make assumptions about people different from you? We all do at times. I would urge you to get to know one individual who stretches you to see reality from a new angle. This is perhaps someone of a different race, religion, or political persuasion, someone from different life circumstances, for example, the homeless. I find that once we connect with a real person, all of our preconceived views about the group they represent quickly vanish.

We all share many of the same hopes, fears, and aspirations. Yet the stock and trade of our political culture today is to exploit and exaggerate differences. We allow fear to drive us into tribes that can easily be manipulated. Lean against fear and embrace our common humanity.

Several years ago, I wrote a tongue-in-cheek article for the *Washington Post* about the intense partisan divides in Washington. I laid blame for this on the cost of housing in this most wealthy of areas. Members of Congress simply cannot afford to live here. In former days, members moved their families to DC and became a vital part of Washington life. A by-product of this was the building of rich relationships outside of politics. In more recent years, members' families remain back in their home districts while the members commute, spending only several days per week in DC. You might recall that House speaker Paul Ryan slept on his office couch while serving in Congress. And since members no longer count one another as friends, it is easier to vilify the "other." Hence the poisonous climate.

An old friend of mine, Senator Bill Nelson, from Florida, was the second member of Congress to go into space. As he peered from that spaceship window, gazing upon that beautiful blue sphere that is our small planet, he wondered how we could fight over so many trivial things, when we all occupy space on this tiny ball in the midst of infinity. What we have in common with others is far greater than what divides us.

Today in the political realm, the environment often feels toxic, yet it is possible to establish deep trust through friendship. At the Department of State, I had the opportunity to work with a remarkable leader, the late John C. Whitehead, former senior partner and chair of Goldman Sachs and later Deputy Secretary of State. One muggy summer morning, as I headed to Capitol Hill to testify with Secretary Whitehead, he lamented about the poisonous atmosphere in Washington. He said, "On Wall Street, people might stab you in the back, but here they say nice things to you until the cameras roll and then stab you in the front." I took a risk and mentioned that there were public figures in Washington who embraced a different bipartisan model rooted in trust and friendship at its core. Whitehead was curious.

So I organized a breakfast for Whitehead. I invited several senators, including Republican Pete Domenici, from New Mexico, Senator and Budget Committee Chair, and his Democratic counterpart, Senator Lawton Chiles, from Florida. When we sat down together, the senators spoke about the importance of investing in friendships across partisan divides. These friendships had enabled them to trust one another and get things done.

Later that week, Whitehead called me. He had just seen Domenici and Chiles arguing over budget matters on C-Span, and yet he knew that behind the scenes there was a profound level of trust, the kind of regard that would enable them to craft compromises. When Chiles had a severe heart attack, glued to his bedside throughout this difficult ordeal was his close pal and confidant Pete Domenici, rooting and praying for his recovery.

Secretary Whitehead was moved. He wanted to be part of a similar small group of people who carved out time to grow and think together. The very next week, Whitehead and I arranged to meet with the Chair of the Joint Chiefs of Staff General David Jones and Senator Charles Percy, from Illinois, along with several others to begin our version of a small support group of friends. The group continues to this day. We discuss our personal challenges and hopes, all within a spiritual context of confidentiality. This is an unusual gathering, since the group is drawn from both believers and "seekers" of all political persuasions, all earnestly looking for an experience and context as a counterpoint to the isolation inherent in positions with demanding responsibilities.

It can seem too simplistic to look at the daunting challenges of our time and think that simple friendship might be a solution to so much mistrust. Yet although it might not be the whole answer, it is surely a central feature in crafting a proven way forward. Whether you are looking for allies to connect with in your professional endeavors or reaching out to supposed political adversaries, the key ingredient is the same: *spend time together with no agenda, share, and learn to be real friends.* Maintaining friendships gives meaning to our lives.

Friendship exposes us to our core, but the risk is well worth taking. If we are lucky, we can all point to moments when friends stood with us through a difficult season. *Networking* seems utterly superficial when compared to the genuine article.

I once observed an extraordinary model of friendship between diplomats from Austria. Parliamentarian Josef Höchtl and the Austrian foreign minister Alois Mock had a problem. The minister's health and memory were clearly failing, but no one was willing to convey such a difficult truth to this distinguished leader. It was crucial, however, to let him know, for the sake of the nation as well as for him personally. Growing numbers of citizens were concerned.

My friend Josef enlisted the help of the head of the largest Austrian television station. He asked for excerpts from Alois's press conferences over the past fifteen years. The clips provided clear evidence of a decline in his friend's cognitive functioning. During a private dinner arranged between these two old, trusted friends, Josef showed the film clips to Alois, evidencing the sad reality of his situation. Josef was unsettled and nervous, yet he felt the risk was necessary. He believed that their deep friendship could withstand the discomfort of an honest conversation. As the footage appeared on the screen, the decline in the foreign minister was unmistakable, even to him. It was an emotional time for two good friends. They wept together and then discussed a viable plan for his care, including the right medical protocol to pursue.

When I ponder this unique friendship between my two Austrian friends, I think of how Dinah Craik described such a tender relationship in *A Life for a Life*: "Oh, the comfort—the inexpressible comfort of feeling *safe* with a person—having neither to weigh thoughts nor measure words, but pouring them all right out, just as they are, chaff and grain together; certain that a faithful hand will take and sift them, keep what is worth keeping, and then with the breath of kindness blow the rest away."[15] A true friend views you in total, your failings and strengths, remembering them all and loving you still.

Find a Great Mentor

Mentoring, a relationship in which a more knowledgeable person guides a less experienced one in a certain area of expertise, is a tradition as old as humankind. The term derives from the ancient text *The Odyssey*, in which Odysseus places his son, Telemachus, in the care of an old family friend, Mentor, to offer him support and guidance while Odysseus is away fighting in the Trojan War. Mentoring is a different manifestation of friendship, because of the teaching and guiding element, the passing on of knowledge.

A great mentor will change your life. In high school, I had the good fortune of meeting Chuck Reinhold. Chuck was a youth leader who had great appeal to young men like me. Chuck was handsome, funny, smart, and a great athlete, having played on the nationally ranked Pitt football team with Mike Ditka. Chuck became my mentor and friend. In fact, Chuck taught me the value of unconditional love in a relationship. He showed me that faith could be robust and masculine, yet kind. He was always there for me, encouraging me, challenging me, and exposing me to people and ideas that expanded my horizons in ways unimaginable to a seventeen-year-old. Chuck was my first mentor. In essence, he became my life coach, guiding me to play the game better, providing both encouragement and challenge. Good coaches do that.

We all need mentors, no matter how successful we've become. Coach K is the legendary men's basketball coach at Duke University. As a University of North Carolina alum, it is difficult for me to applaud anything Duke-related, and yet Coach K is truly an exceptional individual. Coach K once told me a story about him and Michael Jordan. Jordan is arguably the best basketball player of all time (and a UNC graduate, of course).

Coach K served as assistant coach for the 1992 Olympic "dream team," and Jordan was one of his elite players. After one practice, Jordan asked Coach K to remain after practice for a bit. Coach K assumed that the "great one" merely needed an assistant to snag balls for him as he shot around. When the two were alone on the practice court, Jordan said, "Coach, you understand the mechanics of the jump shot better than anyone in the game. Would you observe my shot? I want to get better." The finest basketball player on the planet was seeking to improve and reached for personal coaching. We all need coaches despite our accomplishments.

I worry for the next generation in the business world, especially of young men. Many are in search of mentors but are hard pressed to find any. In our 24/7, nonstop world, older men simply seem too busy to invest in the lives of younger employees. Also, many corporate mentors worry that if they invest in the lives of younger professionals, they are training the competition, since millennials regularly move from job to job. In earlier times, it was considered part of your role to give back to the next generation. Yet many young people today find themselves without engaged fathers and mothers and without mentors actively contributing to their lives. As a result, many seem lost.

If you are experienced in some area, I encourage you to make a regular habit of investing in those with less skill or experience. A mentoring relationship may evolve. If you're in need of training and experience, don't be afraid to seek out a mentor. Look for someone who has something to teach, someone who embodies what you aspire to be. Then be brave and vulnerable and ask for help. You might be surprised at how willing most are to share their wisdom and experience.

Jump Right In

Relationships are central to life. Without deep relationships, our spirits and bodies decline. Yet there is little training in how to be a friend. It is more art than science—but important things are like that. How do you define *love*, *trust*, and *honor*, for instance? Still, we know how critical they are to our well-being.

The best way to establish a genuine friendship is to invest in the relationship. Take a risk. Dare to be really vulnerable and known. Share a weakness. Join a group. Reach across the aisle. Look for guidance. Be willing to share your wisdom. Be open to the possibility of a connection. And once you have committed to participation, be willing to put in the time it will take for the relationship to grow.

So who might be a candidate for your friendship? Don't look for those without faults or without a history of failure; they simply don't exist. The best friends in life are just like you and me—deeply flawed and longing for wholeness and connection.

Find someone willing to share with you their broken parts and wonderings as well as their victories. We're programmed to seek out perfection and to project strength and consistency. Yet the truth is that we don't qualify to be a good friend unless we acknowledge shortcomings. An authentic Navajo rug has one clear imperfection woven into the intricate pattern. The Western mind longs for order, logic, and perfection, whereas Semitic, Native, and Eastern minds are much more comfortable with mystery, paradox, and imperfection.

Embracing our own brokenness prepares us to be a good friend, an approachable friend. Again, be brave, and share who you really are. It is worth the risk. Meaning awaits.

Author and scholar C. S. Lewis raises the stakes on friendship. He sees other mortals through a divine lens:

It is a serious thing to live in a society of possible gods and goddesses, to remember that the dullest and most

uninteresting person you talk to may one day be a creature which, if you saw it now, you would be strongly
tempted to worship. . . . There are no *ordinary* people.
You have never talked to a mere mortal.[16]

Simple friendship is the antidote to our national struggle
with loneliness generally and among leaders in particular.
But it will require an investment of time, heart, and vulnerability. If you make the investment, you will live longer and
have a more satisfying journey.

TAKE ACTION:
Developing and Maintaining Your Relationships

**Americans are lonely. Across the country
almost one out of every two adults—no
matter their race or gender—say they
sometimes or always feel alone or left out.**
**—DAVID M. CORDANI,
PRESIDENT AND CEO, CIGNA**

In your journal reflect on these questions and exercises:

• *What is a friend? Did your parents have friends?*

• *Why is it important to cultivate friendships? Can
successful people have trusted friends?*

- *Do you feel isolated? And if so, what contributed to that?*

- *What scares you about being vulnerable in a relationship? Who have you been vulnerable with in your life? How did those experiences go?*

- *Do you trust easily? Have you been betrayed by a friend? How do your experiences of trust affect you today?*

- *Describe the ideal friendship. Do you have any friendships that come close to that ideal? Who are you an ideal friend to?*

Make Gratitude a Regular Practice

> I would maintain that thanks are the
> highest form of thought; and that gratitude
> is happiness doubled by wonder.
>
> —G. K. CHESTERTON, ENGLISH ESSAYIST

> The more of an effort you make to feel gratitude
> one day, the more the feeling will come to you
> spontaneously in the future. . . . Gratitude can spiral:
> the more thankful we feel, the more likely we are to
> act pro-socially toward others, causing *them* to feel
> grateful and setting up a beautiful virtuous cascade.
>
> —CHRISTIAN JARRETT, BRITISH NEUROSCIENTIST

So how does having a grateful outlook toward life contribute to a life of meaning? Remember when your grandmother would urge you to "count your blessings"? Well, it turns out that grandma was right, and her advice is backed by rigorous research conducted by neuroscientists and psychologists.

But let's keep this simple for the moment. Why is it important to take the time to count our blessings? Simply put, we have no need to list the things that suck in our lives. We know them well. These are the things that wake us at three o'clock in the morning, that we fret about as we open the second bottle of Caymus. The real trick is *focus*. By regularly and consciously identifying very specific things for which we are grateful, our attitudes and brain actually change. It works and enables us to view life and reality in a much different manner.

Writing thank-you notes, keeping gratitude lists, and literally counting our blessings help make us more optimistic and happier than those who don't have such practices. But the payoff doesn't end there. Researchers Robert Emmons and Michael McCullough found that those who practiced gratefulness got more and better sleep and exercised more than control groups.[1]

Researchers at Temple University conducted an experiment in which hyper-intensive patients were divided into two groups. Both groups received medical treatments, but one group was asked to phone a gratitude hotline, recalling for the eager listeners specific things for which they were thankful. The callers noticed physical improvements. Their blood pressure decreased more than the control group, who only had medical treatment.[2] Gratitude is a balm, physically and mentally.

Most of the research on gratitude has focused on adults. But researchers are shifting attention to the benefits of this practice for children as well. Adolescents who rate higher in gratitude tend to be happier and more engaged scholastically and have far fewer depressive symptoms and less anxiety and antisocial behavior than less grateful peers. The research goes on to say there are implications for adolescents who have gone astray, finding that growth in gratitude over four years is predictive of prosocial behavior and a marked decrease in negative tendencies.[3]

The practice of making a gratitude list shifts our focus, enabling us to home in on what's good and positive in life rather than what's going wrong. As a critical aspect of their job, airline pilots rely on various checklists to improve "situational awareness." The lists are designed to ensure that pilots never miss what's central to their mission. The medical world is applying similar protocols to health care, to avoid slipups and malpractice suits. Shouldn't we take the same care with our personal lives? The ingredients that contribute to the rich stew of meaning are knowable. By creating checklists that prompt us to dwell on the simple yet wondrous all around, rather than the dark and hopeless, we are happier and feel more alive.

Start with Three Thank-Yous

Each morning, I make it a practice to write down at least three things for which I am grateful. While alone in these early hours, I might record that I'm grateful for a roof over my head, good health, an unexpected call from a friend the previous day, or that delicious mug of dark Italian roast coffee on my side table.

Often the things I register are basic and unremarkable. Still, I have a sense of calm when I look back on such prosaic delights.

By year's end, I have a list of hundreds of small bursts of wonder and goodness that contribute to a positive state of mind. On December 31, I clip the page, laminate it, and save it for future review. Perhaps it will inspire my three sons to do something similar.

You can go into more depth through the use of a private journal. Writing by hand is particularly beneficial; it slows you down so you have to consider your thoughts and helps still that internal mental engine that ceaselessly runs within. My journal is a quiet companion. Just looking at it brings me a sense of peace. And writing about an issue or problem offers space and perspective to make decisions that I might not have made, had I not slowed things down and considered various options.

Have you noticed that when someone just listens to our problem, even when no concrete answers are offered, a sense of relief comes over us? There's something about naming an issue or problem that brings peace and clarity. A journal is useful in that respect as well. By just describing a challenge, we can feel a sense of freedom and relief. You'll enjoy a broader sense of well-being as you take stock of matters and quietly reflect. In essence, you've moved the problem from your gut to a piece of paper. Just naming things gives us power over the problem. God's first charge to Adam was to name the animals.[4] To the ancient Hebrews, naming represented power over another.

Motivated leaders attack problems relentlessly, reaching for quick fixes that might or might not work. Sometimes we think this strategy will work in our personal lives as well—but often it does not. Obsessive focus upon our problems can become a destructive habit, an emotional cul-de-sac that is hard to exit and harms our health and sense of well-being.

An ancient saying warns, "You become what you think about." You're not what *you* think you are but what you *think* you are. The mind is powerful. It needs a focus. Quiet journaling helps reset our minds, enabling us to focus upon our larger purpose and the blessings of this life. A journal containing lots of inspired thoughts, notes, lists of thanksgivings, and quotations can serve to fill your mind with a fresh outlook and enable renewal. This practice has proved beneficial to many throughout the ages.

Rather than bringing a problem-solving business mindset to our personal lives, how about doing the reverse? What if we applied a gratitude mindset to our work context? Yes, I understand, it is easier to notice what's not working rather than what is. But how about viewing your employees with a different eye, an eye of appreciation and gratitude? Identify what you value in your colleagues and be very specific about their behaviors and attitudes. You've likely never told them such things. They will probably be surprised to learn that you have even noticed their positive traits. Experiment with this. It changes everything.

Several years ago, I read a simple book, *The One Minute Manager*, by Kenneth Blanchard and Spencer Johnson, that had a novel approach to managing employees. The authors presented a compelling yet straightforward vision for leading an organization or a team.[5] Rather than catching people screwing up and doing the wrong things (a very human tendency), leaders should catch them doing what's right and positive for the organization. It is far easier to notice the negative and to give it your energy and focus. They argued that if you praise employees for their accomplishments, it builds on itself and creates an energized and uplifting work environment. They'll become great allies in helping shape a positive corporate culture of trust and possibility. They'll emulate such practices with their own teams. Your new approach will spread organically. But it starts at the top, not with mere sloganeering but with concrete daily reinforcement.

Someone who employed this approach of "catching someone doing the right thing" was the legendary coach of the Dallas Cowboys, Tom Landry. While other coaches reviewed countless hours of failed tackles and other blatant mistakes with players, Landry took a different approach. For each of his players, Landry created a highlight reel of the man's greatest plays—good blocks, effective tackles, successful runs, or amazing catches, all done at the highest level. His rationale was that the mistakes were obvious and ever present in players' minds, but recalling what was done naturally, correctly, or to great effect took effort. Therefore, Landry simply reminded them of their greatness, urging them to simply draw upon those past successes and repeat them. Coach Landry told each of his players on day one, "We only replay your winning plays."

Top marriage and relationship researcher John Gottman

found that to offset every negative interaction in any relationship, you need five constructive interactions.[6] Is it any wonder
that our work environments are so toxic, with our incessant
preoccupation with the negative? We can tip that balance by
developing a new ethos, by elevating gratitude above criticism, spotlighting the good, and telling stories that reinforce
a genuine culture of constructive change and encouragement.

This approach also makes good business sense. Employee
recruitment and training are costly for companies. If employees stay longer, the bottom line is enhanced. Employees long to
be a part of organizations perceived as valuing them as human
beings and contributors. Consider the examples of Southwest
Airlines, Trader Joe's, Costco, Delta, and others who make employee satisfaction the very first priority. All are leaders in their
respective sectors. Employees are proud to work at such organizations. Who wouldn't prefer that kind of culture?

A Tool in Dark Times

All over the world, there are special people who have endured
unimaginable adversity and have every reason to be bitter,
yet chose to think differently. Young Fatima Arabzada, whom
I know, was just such a person. She's from Afghanistan, yet
grew up in Iran. At age ten, she was relocated to a refugee
camp. But instead of living a life of despair, she started a radio
station with a sister and a girlfriend. They wanted to share

positive stories with other young Afghans. This, in turn, led her and her sister to start two other initiatives that were beacons of light in a dark and often futile environment. Fatima didn't allow her situation to define her and prevent her from making a positive difference against all odds. We all have that opportunity if we will just seize it. It takes practice to deviate from patterns that hold us captive, yet possibilities await.

Trust me, each of us has ample justification for disappointment and anger. After all, as your mother insisted, "Life is not fair." As we have experienced life, most of us have been hurt, judged, and betrayed along the way. We can transcend harsh blows and setbacks by establishing a personal habit of simple gratitude.

If you're grateful, you can face hardship courageously and positively. In fact, you might discover, during the most difficult of times, a strength and resilience you might not have otherwise been aware of. Consider New York Yankees baseball star Lou Gehrig. On July 4, 1939, Gehrig approached the microphone between the two games of a doubleheader at Yankee Stadium. Standing in front of sixty thousand adoring fans, Gehrig gave an emotional speech. He thanked the fans for their kindness and encouragement. He had been diagnosed with ALS (amyotrophic lateral sclerosis), a devastating degenerative disease. At thirty-six, he was only expected to live a few more years at most and with a quality of life that would be severely diminished over time.

Still, what stood out to him on that clear Manhattan day was the life he had been privileged to live and the love that he had received from fans, teammates, and family. He stood there in that fabled ballpark, with greats like Babe Ruth by his side, and uttered something that made the crowd go silent. He declared that he was "the luckiest man on the face of the earth." This dying man demonstrated humility and gratitude in the face of irreversible tragedy. He was thankful for the outpouring of love that arose from his death sentence.

Have you ever thanked someone who was there for you during a challenging time? Don't put it off.

Grateful people are able to see beyond what's troubling in the moment. Former president Ronald Reagan saw beyond his deteriorating health condition to appreciate and celebrate an extraordinary life of service. He wrote a letter to the American people on November 4, 1994, alerting them of his worsening Alzheimer's condition and the burden that his dear Nancy would surely bear. His last words in the letter are particularly memorable: "In closing, let me thank you, the American people, for giving me the great honor of allowing me to serve as your president. . . . I now begin the journey that will lead me into the sunset of my life. I know that for America there will always be a bright dawn ahead." Reagan wasn't bitter about his diagnosis, a condition that he knew would rob him of his faculties. He was focused more on the trust that was accorded him as president of the United States. His words of simple gratitude were moving and memorable.

During the Dutch Resistance, Corrie ten Boom was arrested and placed in a Nazi concentration camp for harboring Jews in Amsterdam. One of the daily annoyances in their sparse dormitory was the presence of bedbugs. They added to the daily list of horrors faced by these brave people. While praying one day, ten Boom decided to be grateful for those wretched pests. Even she was surprised at this decision. Unexpectedly, days later her captors decided to no longer inspect their dormitory—because of the bedbugs! With no oversight, ten Boom and her fellow prisoners could have conversations and a level of freedom unimaginable just days earlier. Thank God for bedbugs! As Thornton Wilder wrote in *The Woman of Andros* in 1930: "We can only be said to be alive in those moments when our hearts are conscious of our treasures."

Perhaps one of the most remarkable things about Gehrig and Reagan is that they were confronted with the worst. In the face of death, both men focused on their good fortunes. Imagine if your life as you knew it was shattered at a young age. Could you pick up the pieces and find a way forward?

I went to high school with a champion athlete, Joni Eareckson. Her senior year, Joni had a diving accident, broke her neck, and was paralyzed from the neck down. After a long convalescence and much soul searching, Joni emerged with a surprising outlook filled with gratitude and purpose. Incredibly, she put her tragedy to good use. She became a happy warrior for the disabled. She learned to paint holding a brush in her mouth. She married. She recorded a successful pop album and became a bestselling author. A film was made of her life story.

During a private moment with her, I asked, "Joni, you have said publicly that you can't imagine being more fulfilled than you are now, though you are totally paralyzed. Is that really true?"

She beamed and said, "I am so grateful for each day. Yes! Yes! Yes!"

There are only two choices when faced with an unthinkable reality: succumb to bitterness or adjust your thinking, reimagine your purpose, and view matters in a larger context rooted in thanksgiving. As a friend once said to me, "You get either bitter or better." Joni became better.

It's essential to cultivate gratitude as a habit. You may not have to deal with the adversity that Eareckson, Gehrig, Reagan, and Arabzada have faced; they serve as inspirational guides, nonetheless.

Reflect on your current circumstances. What's your temperament? Do you get angry and bitter when setbacks or even small slights present themselves? You can alter your brain chemistry by resisting those ingrained ways of thinking. Wallowing in cynicism and bitterness is not a good health regime. Build a new history and routine. Start small. Take note of life's little blessings. Name and celebrate the positive, despite what comes your way.

Find Time for Reflection

In the previous chapter, we explored the value and necessity of establishing relationships. But do you realize that times of

solitude and quiet materially enhance the quality of those relationships? And do you also know that solitude creates space
for gratitude?

Socrates challenged, "Beware the barrenness of a busy
life." Unfortunately, most of us don't view alone time in a positive way and seek to fill the void with activity and noise. Blaise
Pascal understood it best. He believed that our lack of solitude is at the heart of our emptiness: "The sole cause of man's
unhappiness is that he does not know how to stay quietly in
his room."[7]

I came across an alarming study published in *Science*
magazine several years ago. University of Virginia psychologists asked a group of students to sit quietly with no distractions for six to fifteen minutes. Most hated the experience
and found it extremely difficult and unsettling. But wait, it
gets even worse. Researchers expanded the study to include
a wider range of backgrounds and ages and this time provided a means of distraction. Those in the study were left in
a room that was empty except for a device that would deliver
a painful electric shock if the silence proved untenable for
them. The findings: one-fourth of the women and two-thirds
of the men shocked themselves during a fifteen-minute period. For many, any stimulation, even if painful, was prefer-
able to alone time.[8]

But solitude is essential and provides the space to reflect
upon our lives, relationships, challenges, and, yes, blessings.
The poet Rumi said it this way, "There is a voice that doesn't

use words. Listen." Running and striving preclude perceiving the truly wonderous. Our instinct is to focus on the problems before us. We need time to reflect in order to recall all that's good about our lives. The people I meet who have a regular practice of quiet reflection are far more grounded and grateful than others. Correlated? I believe so. It's disturbing to find that the very thing we need to feed our souls is something we avoid at all costs.

Each January, I join fifteen accomplished leaders for a three-day silent retreat at a Trappist monastery in the rolling Virginia countryside. It is bitterly cold at that time of year, as we step back in time to join a community of monks whose entire approach to life may seem antiquated and irrelevant to the challenges of our day. But for we who gather, it is a powerful life-changing experience. To be with others, but alone, is initially challenging but becomes comfortable with practice. We eat together, walk together, but never speak. At the end of our three days of seclusion, we share among ourselves any lessons and insights gained from this time of disengagement and quiet. We emerge from this ritual of time apart as more confident and grounded individuals.

Solitude differs from loneliness. Solitude fills our hearts with gratitude and renewed energy for living. Loneliness kills our very souls and often spirals into sadness and despair. Although they might look similar on the surface, the comparison ends there. I would urge that you consider starting a solitude practice. Your outlook will improve measurably.

Rewire Your Brain

It's easy to be grateful when we are happy and things are going well. But as we all know, those times don't last forever. The trick is to be grateful in both good times and bad, all seasons of our lives. As individuals and as a society, we are guided by our deepest obsessions. If our thoughts are constantly full of fear and scarcity, we become afraid of losing everything. Ironically, if we are grateful, even in the darkest of times, we become more hopeful.

Gratitude makes us believe in the future. It's a bit like slalom skiing. To exert control, you must lean down the hill, but that is frightening. It is counterintuitive and challenges common sense and yet it is true; by leaning forward into your fear, with gratitude, you actually have far greater control. Yes, it feels safer to lean back rather than forward, because it is a familiar response, born of sheer terror, whether on the ski slopes or in life. We lean back in life, fearing the adventure ahead, holding on to the need to settle scores, and listing our wrongs and "what-ifs." As many of us know too well, that path leads to a dead end. Let go. Be grateful and set a new focus. Slowly learn a new dance, a much more human way of living life.

Once you change your focus to what you are thankful for, life is seen as a gift. As someone once said, "Life is not about the number of breaths we take, but the number of moments that take our breath away." You were given the gift of life, but there are no assurances. Any moment could be your last.

Don't take anything for granted, and eventually you'll craft a life approach anchored in gratitude and resulting in real joy.

David Brooks points out that there are people with "dispositional gratitude," meaning they are grateful by nature most of the time. They stand in stark contrast to those who are entitled. Brooks reflects, "People with grateful dispositions see their efforts grandly but not themselves. Life doesn't surpass their dreams but it nicely surpasses their expectations."[9]

What stands out to you about your day so far? Or the past month? Or year? Are you clinging to something that's pulling you down? Where's your attention focused? What we focus on matters.

Daniel Simons and Christopher Chabris conducted a famous study on attention at Harvard. They produced a short video that featured two teams, one dressed in black and the other in white. The players in the film clip simply passed a basketball back and forth among themselves, and the Harvard students were instructed to watch the short video and count the number of passes made by the players in white uniforms. Following the experiment, the students were asked if they noticed anything odd in the video. More than half of the observers failed to notice a large furry gorilla walking among the two teams while they were passing the ball.[10]

How could they miss something so obvious? The truth is, we only see what we pay attention to. So if you're fixated on darkness, then that's all you will see. You'll miss out on the light and the causes for wonder all around.

Grateful people thrive because they pay attention to the right things. Paul Dolan observes, in *Happiness by Design*, that it is important to acknowledge the cause of your happiness. He notes, "The key to being happier is to pay more attention to what makes you happy and less attention to what does not. Notice this is not the same as paying attention to happiness itself."[11]

It's important to note that happiness is only a by-product of something far more important. Our goal should be to have a life of meaning. I draw a distinction between happiness and meaning. Happiness is tied to circumstances and the externalities in our lives (getting a promotion at work, losing nineteen pounds, having a great weekend, etc.). Deep meaning is utterly profound and not necessarily dependent on any externalities. It is a sense of well-being that resides within and does not correlate with our shifting circumstances. Although deep within, it is also transcendent and spiritual in nature. This is why, in some of the darkest times, like serving a life sentence in jail or enduring a horrific war, certain people still manage to find a connection to meaning.

A note found in the pocket of a fallen Confederate soldier gives voice to this seeming contradiction between happiness and meaning:

> *I asked for strength that I might achieve;*
> *I was made weak that I might learn humbly to obey.*
> *I asked for health that I might do greater things;*
> *I was given infirmity that I might do better things.*

I asked for riches that I might be happy;
I was given poverty that I might be wise.
I asked for power that I might have the praise of men;
I was given weakness that I might feel the need of God.
I asked for all things that I might enjoy life;
I was given life that I might enjoy all things.
I got nothing that I asked for, but everything I had hoped for.
Almost despite myself, my unspoken prayers were answered;
I am, among all men, most richly blessed.

It's easy to dismiss and trivialize small shifts and practices that slowly generate human flourishing. If that is your tendency, I urge you to reconsider and take up the disciplined practice of counting your blessings. It's an investment in you.

Adjustments in your focus make room for the possibility of meaning and joy.

TAKE ACTION:
Making Gratitude a Regular Practice

Want to be happy? Be grateful.

—DAVID STEINDL-RAST, BENEDICTINE MONK

In your journal reflect on these questions and exercises:

• *Write down ten specific things, large or small, for which you are grateful.*

- *Were your parents or caregivers grateful people? Who do you know who is grateful? How do these role models influence your practice of gratitude?*

- *For five consecutive days, record daily two to five things for which you are thankful. Small things are just fine.*

- *Write a handwritten note or letter to someone thanking them for the role they have played in your life or for something specific they did for you in the past.*

- *Notice a colleague's specific work product or attitude and let that person know how it affected you.*

- *Catch your child or other family member doing something right, acknowledge it, and perhaps celebrate it.*

- *Think of some service provider in your life—a checkout clerk, plumber, house cleaner, etc.—and write them a note thanking them for what they do for you; enclose a monetary gift.*

- *Write a thank-you note weekly for one month, thanking special people in your life.*

- *Name five things you have noticed from the above exercises about the practical benefits of practicing gratitude.*

Learn to Forgive and Serve

**Before you embark on a journey of
revenge, dig two graves.**
—Confucius

**Altruism and compassion are vital components
of personal, economic, environmental, and social
change. Altruism can be the guiding principle
leading us all to live better, and the good news is that
it is a dimension we all possess and can cultivate.**
**—Matthieu Ricard,
cell biologist and Buddhist monk**

Two important themes essential to thriving are forgiveness and care for others. We could explore both separately, devoting a chapter to each, but I have chosen to look at them together, since there are important synergies between the two. At the most basic level, if you are bitter and unwilling to forgive, you are not in a healthy position to focus on others' concerns and needs. Instead, your gaze is inward; you are busy nursing and seeking to justify your anger and inner turmoil. Living a life of grievance like this, you are unable to care about or even notice the needs of those around you. All of us can find ample justification to cling to our private hurt and anger, envisioning settling the score or worse.

We do not forgive because others deserve it. We forgive because it is important for our souls. Forgiving frees us to get on with our lives and to experience a meaning derived from loving and caring for others. So selfless caring actually starts with forgiveness, both of others and of ourselves. UC–Davis scholar Robert Emmons observes: "You cannot be grateful and resentful at the same time, or forgiving and vengeful."[1] It's all connected.

It has been said that not forgiving is like drinking poison and expecting another to die; it is pointless and utterly self-destructive. In an article for the *New York Times* called "The Futility of Vengeance," Kate Murphy tells of a vengeful Harvard professor who "harassed the owner of a family-run Chinese restaurant for triple monetary damages after a mistaken $4 overcharge."[2]

Murphy also points to an Australian entrepreneur who exemplifies the delight so many find in random acts of vengeance. The entrepreneur created a unique service that enables you to send an enemy an envelope containing small bits of sparkly glitter. When the unsuspecting subject of your wrath opens the envelope, the glitter explodes everywhere, creating a mess that's virtually impossible to clean up. Murphy notes, "A rush of customers crashed the company's website within 24 hours."[3] A vengeful burst of glitter isn't overtly violent or damaging, but it's still a form of retaliation fueled by a lack of forgiveness—and it doesn't stop once the vengeful action has been undertaken.

Allen Kurzweil spent decades working to get even with the bully who made his elementary-school life utterly miserable. In his widely publicized memoir, *Whipping Boy: The Forty-Year Search for My Twelve-Year-Old Bully*, Kurzweil details his bully's many adult failings and legal woes.[4] I can only imagine what it did to Kurzweil to nurse those slights for so many decades. Let's be honest. We all quietly enjoy it when someone is outed for bad behavior, particularly someone who has hurt or slighted us. The Germans even have a word for it: schadenfreude—"delight at the misfortune of others." What a great word!

One of the funniest films I have ever watched is *What About Bob?* It features hilarious interactions between Dr. Leo Marvin, a pompous insecure Boston psychiatrist, played by Richard Dreyfuss, and his unruly patient, Bob Wiley, played by Bill Murray. When Dr. Marvin's book *Baby Steps* accidentally brings prominence to his patient Bob rather than to himself, the therapist devolves into ever darker levels of revenge seeking. It is a humorous over-the-top caricature of the slippery slope and toxic effects of resentment and unforgiveness gone awry. Dr. Marvin desperately wants to destroy his patient. In fact, he delights in so doing.

All of these illustrations underscore one main point: unforgiveness is toxic and paralyzing and sabotages our lives. It can control our thinking in unhealthy ways.

But forgiveness? Forgiveness can heal, offer hope, and provide a way forward. Consider the power of forgiveness on display within a close-knit Amish community in rural Pennsylvania in 2006. Two unimaginable acts occurred within the span of a few weeks that year. The first act was horrific. Charles Roberts, a quiet milkman, killed five young Amish girls between the ages of six and thirteen and injured five others in a shooting rampage. The shooter concluded this nightmare by killing himself.

The second unimaginable act occurred a week or so later at a small Methodist church in that same small town. Of the mourners gathered for Roberts's funeral service, half were Amish. These people of faith came to support the widow of the shooter and her three small children. They offered money and encouragement to the stunned and grieving family and, most especially, forgiveness for a senseless act that robbed a tiny, close-knit community of innocent children. They could reach out and love the unlovable, because they first forgave.

Right behavior begins with right thinking. If you hold a philosophy or theology that values forgiveness, it enables and empowers you to forgive, even in the most challenging of circumstances. This simple Amish community stunned the world by behaving in accord with its beliefs. It is a powerful testimonial. It should make us all pause to consider: What do we believe? Does it animate our lives in concrete ways? If not, what's the use?

True forgiveness is undeserved and takes your breath

away when you experience it up close. At the bail hearing on June 19, 2015, in Charleston, South Carolina, for the Mother Emanuel Church killer, family members who had suffered grievous loss at the hands of the disaffected young white supremacist stood before him in that stark government holding room. Each congregant who spoke conveyed a surprisingly consistent sentiment: forgiveness.

Nadine Collier's mother, Ethel Lance, was killed on that tragic evening. Nadine Collier told the shooter, Dylann Roof, "I forgive you. You took something very precious away from me. . . . You hurt me. You hurt a lot of people. If God forgives you, I forgive you."[5]

How do such people marshal the inner resources to forgive on such an epic scale? Congressman Mark Sanford, who represents Charleston, witnessed the public hearing in person. Mark is a close friend of mine. He flew back to Washington and joined me for dinner that evening. He was overwhelmed and deeply moved by the grace extended to Roof at the sentencing hearing. Again, it was an inspiring case of belief put to the test.

These acts of forgiveness are awe-inspiring and, for many of us, unfathomable. Forgiveness takes practice. And forgiveness begins small. We shouldn't try to forgive ISIS or the Nazis, who murdered over six million Jews. We should start by forgiving Uncle Harry's obnoxious son who picks his nose and trashes our basement.

There is actual data to back up the notion of starting with

bite-size actions to effect change. In his book *The Power of Habit*, author Charles Duhigg illustrates how addictions were successfully broken by slowly cobbling together slight shifts in behavior rather than by trying to boil the ocean or design some mega-action plan.[6] For forgiveness to become a habit and not just a one-off occurrence, we need to integrate it into our daily routine.

It is one thing to extend forgiveness and another to ask for it. *Washington Post* columnist and friend Michael Gerson recalled a story from his time as chief speechwriter for George W. Bush in 2000. Gerson was with the president in the family theater as the president prepared for his first address to Congress. A military operator had been tasked with making sure the teleprompter operated properly, but the young tech messed up. Bush stormed out, declaring, "Call me when you get your act together." Several minutes later, clearly chastened, the president reentered the room and apologized. "That is not the way the president of the United States should act," he said. The young soldier was taken with the leader's genuine humility.[7]

Whether you are the president of the United States or an average citizen, asking for forgiveness is hard, requiring a contrite spirit. It's never easy to admit you were wrong; our pride looms large. This likely accounts for C. S. Lewis's view that simple pride is by far the worst sin and stands in the way of forgiving.

By their early teens, my two oldest boys were establishing their talented band, the Epochs. I was certainly proud but also concerned about the darker aspects of the music business, a world I didn't understand. After a late-night show in DC on 14th Street, I observed my fourteen-year-old negotiating a band fee with a Rastafarian who seemed whacked out on drugs. I felt a profound sense of dread, but had no idea where to go with that feeling. I was eager for this stage of their life and artistic expression to come to an end and for them to find a different, more conventional path.

Soon after that, I had lunch with Terry Golden, then CEO of the Host Marriott Corporation, in Rockville, Maryland. Terry has two adult boys, one in the music business and the other in finance. I thought, "Wow, this is my chance to glean some wisdom on how to guide my boys away from what seems an increasingly perilous course." And after all, Terry had a son who was a drummer in a rock band.

As I poured out my heart, all the fear and anxiety spilled out. He listened intently before he responded with three observations. First he said that it didn't appear that the boys were involved in anything risky or life-threatening. Then he pointed out that it's rare for anyone to discover a true passion. Finally he said, "They are different from you, and perhaps you are struggling with that fact." The third observation cut like a knife. Of course, he was right.

For a long while after leaving that conversation, I sat in the leafy suburban parking lot of the Host Marriott Corporation. I recall it was raining. I then drove home and asked my boys if we might chat. Once settled after an awkward silence, I began, "Often, I have celebrated your musical talent, but I have privately wondered when this chapter of your lives might end.

Frankly, I have been afraid of the entertainment industry and a subculture that is foreign and threatening to me. I was wrong. I would like to ask your forgiveness for not being the champion of your dreams."

Not certain how to respond or what prompted my change of heart, they generously forgave me. It was a simple gesture of contrition, but one that altered my behavior toward their future work in the music world. I truly changed following that moment.

Forgiveness, whether you are forgiving or being forgiven, can alter your life for the better. Now I celebrate each and every achievement in my sons' unique artistic journey. Some years after that talk, my son Hays called me from Manhattan. He was a sophomore at Columbia University studying architecture. He told me that the band had been offered a great opportunity to pursue their music full-time in Seattle. He, his brother, and the band would be handsomely paid. Implicit in the offer was a record deal. Hays asked what I thought, since he was also thriving at this prestigious Ivy League university with a stellar GPA and a bright, professional future in sight.

I didn't hesitate for a moment. "Get out of there," I said. "This is an opportunity of a lifetime. This is your dream. Do it!" Frankly, I was surprised at myself, delighting in their opportunity rather than fearing what this path might entail. What a change in me, and it was real. Forgiveness does that. It is humbling and liberating, creating new possibilities.

I'm finding the more I realize how deeply flawed I am

and accept it, the less I react to criticisms of all sorts. Yet we all become defensive on occasion. Our defenses arise as we are challenged by others. Abraham Lincoln has been such a source of inspiration for me in this regard.

When Abraham Lincoln was president, the press was brutal. Here was a self-taught man from Illinois, not Massachusetts or Virginia, the traditional homes of America's presidents. Lincoln was awkward and clearly not a part of the eastern establishment. In an informal gathering with the press, it is alleged that a sympathetic reporter asked the president how he endured the relentless withering public criticism of his appearance, intelligence, and leadership. Lincoln paused and simply replied, "I'm so much worse than they could ever know."

What a reaction. His humble spirit defused the situation. The truth is that we are all worse than anyone might ever imagine. The more aware we are of our flaws and failings, the more likely we are to respond like Lincoln. The truth is that we all are in need of forgiveness. But the wonder of forgiveness is that the more we see ourselves as we truly are, broken and needy, the more we can treat others with love and empathy. As we forgive ourselves, we are liberated to forgive others.

Modeling Forgiveness

Like so much of our everyday behavior, forgiveness is learned at our parents' knees, typically through observation and personal experience. The same is true of forgiveness's evil twin, resentment. Few of us grew up in families where grace and forgiveness were easily and regularly extended. Many of us observed quite the opposite—ongoing bitterness and anger, and a narrative of retribution that never quite ended. Ice-cold body language and silence belied deep hurt.

It is important to look back, reflect, and evaluate how our family model shaped our views of forgiveness. If we don't understand the story we were born into, as we have discussed earlier, it is likely that we will continue this unfortunate legacy for generations to come. If one of your parents was deeply angry and unforgiving, this is important information, since this early experience shaped you and is likely embedded in your psyche, perhaps requiring some professional counsel or, at a minimum, thoughtful exploration to find liberation and the space to behave differently.

Not forgiving is corrosive to the soul and spirals downward into an inability to trust. One way to open the door to forgiveness is to separate people from their acts. We all do destructive and surprising things on occasion, if we're honest. That doesn't mean we are bad people. We are all grappling with our own humanity, with its hurts and bitter disappointments. On the path to becoming a forgiving person, take a cue from Alcoholics Anonymous and make an honest inventory of your behaviors. AA is famous for gathering those who admit that they are powerless over their addiction. By giving voice to their problems and declaring their inability on their own to stop drinking, people are empowered to begin a journey of transformation and healing. They also benefit from a strong support network of fellow "broken" souls.

It's vital to note that forgiving isn't condoning. Nor does it mean that you are excusing unacceptable behavior. You can strongly disapprove of others' actions and still forgive them for what they have done. It's up to them to decide whether they seek change. Also, you don't have to reconcile with others in order to forgive them completely. Our job is to change what we are able. We have little power over their decisions.

Forgiveness is tied to empathy. It is easier to forgive when you understand the circumstance of the offender. I recall learning that Saddam Hussein lived on the streets of Cairo as a young boy. This certainly does not justify his barbaric behavior, but it helps make sense of his story. The poet Henry Wadsworth Longfellow put it this way: "If we could read the secret history of our enemies, we should find in each man's life sorrow and suffering enough to disarm all hostility." How true.

The eighteenth-century British playwright Hannah More saw forgiveness as the "economy of the heart," because it "saves the expense of anger, the cost of hatred, the waste of spirits." We need to consider if any strategy of clinging to past grievances actually works. We likely need to let go of the crazy notion that by stoking bitterness, we are somehow extracting revenge and evening the score. Oscar Wilde cynically quipped that you should always forgive your enemies, because nothing annoys them more.

Bestselling author Malcolm Gladwell had an epiphany when he sat in Cliff and Wilma Derksens' den in Winnipeg.

Some thirty years earlier, on November 30, 1984, their thirteen-year-old daughter, Candace, had disappeared; her body was discovered seven weeks later in a small structure near the Derksen home. The Derksens' response to the murder and the retrieval of her remains was immediate and shocking: they chose to forgive the perpetrator and told the world so shortly after the grisly murder scene was discovered. "We have all done something dreadful in our lives, or have felt the urge to," Wilma declared.

Gladwell was astounded. How could the Derksens muster such courage in the face of utter evil and cruelty? They relied on their deep Mennonite faith, of which forgiveness is an integral part. The experience was life-changing for Gladwell; it challenged his core beliefs. In the den of a modest bungalow in Canada he found a renewed hope and faith.[8]

In the mid-1990s, I found myself affected by a Ponzi scheme. It was almost unbelievable that so many bright people fell for a story that seemed, in retrospect, too good to be true. I was a minor player in this unfortunate drama, but I knew most of the participants involved. It was a virtual *Who's Who* of Wall Street. The press loved the story, since it made so many accomplished people appear foolish and not so smart after all. As the story evolved, my name got identified with the perpetrator of this foul deed. Perfect!

This was such an awful period for me. During that time I often mused, "How did I get pulled into this?" It was only later that I found out. Two years after this saga ended with the mastermind safely behind bars, I got a call from an acquaintance in New York who asked if we might meet. Two weeks later over sandwiches, he confessed that he had called a senior press official and told him I was involved.

He turned to me while we were eating and said, "I am here to ask your forgiveness. I have been at times jealous of you and wanted to injure you. It was wrong. Will you forgive me?"

Of course, I forgave him. And as I left our luncheon I thought to myself, "Why don't more of us take ownership of our wrongs and ask forgiveness?" I was impressed by the courage he showed to confess and ask forgiveness. We all do harm to others. Forgiveness clears the deck. I still have much work to do.

Individual forgiveness is one thing, but what of the killing fields of Pol Pot or other such atrocities involving the murder of countless innocents? Should some misdeeds never be forgiven?

A case in point is that of Adolf Eichmann, the Nazi most responsible for the killing process that sent so many Jews to their death. In 1961, the young nation of Israel sentenced Eichmann to be executed. This was all the more stunning since Israel had abolished the death penalty in 1954. The philosopher Martin Buber, deeply troubled by this sentence, enlisted the Israeli prime minister, David Ben-Gurion, to seek clemency for Eichmann. Not surprisingly, outrage over the suggestion of forgiveness dominated the public conversation. The newspaper *Maariv* voiced what most Jews felt: "A pardon for Eichmann? No! Six million times no!" Given that the stakes were raised considerably due to the epic scale of the crime, it is easy to understand why the Jews wanted his death. But is there another approach?

It is fascinating to juxtapose the approach that South Africa took to the systemic wrongdoing of apartheid: the establishment, under the leadership of Bishop Desmond Tutu, of the Truth and Reconciliation Commission, which intended to put the racist history of South Africa behind by allowing wrongdoers to confess their crimes, experience forgiveness, and thereby find a way forward, both for them and for the nation. This approach, which was powerful to observe, became a model for other such situations, like the one in Rwanda. Institutional wrongdoing is more challenging for me as I think of forgiveness. But I believe the principle remains the same regardless of the scale of the wrongdoing: forgiveness enables us to find the freedom to move on.

There are limitless opportunities to forgive and to be forgiven. A Franciscan monk told me that when he lived in Cincinnati, he had "70 × 7" painted over the main door of his parish church. Mail carriers often mistook the number for a street address, but it had a far deeper meaning. When Jesus's disciples asked how many times they should forgive when wronged, he told them "seventy times seven," the biblical number for infinity.[9]

There will always be new reasons to forgive those in our universe of relationships, particularly those closest to us. Life is like that—dynamic, never static. Forgiveness should be part of our daily routine. Otherwise, we succumb to bitterness, playing the victim. Again, as Paul exhorted, "Forgiv[e] one another, even as God in Christ forgave you."[10] How humbling and liberating, yet how profoundly difficult to do.

Are You a Giver?

If you have ever been forgiven when you didn't deserve it, you know how you can be overwhelmed by feelings of unworthiness. Yet once fully embraced, the experience generates a corresponding impulse to extend ourselves to others, even those as undeserving as we are. This new outlook can animate our actions and care for others. As givers, we can now see with eyes of compassion and concern.

When I think of givers in my life, Bob Brown is among those who stand tallest. Years ago, Bob put aside his own agenda to assist me in the difficult days of apartheid in South Africa. Bob grew up in the segregated South, stood with Martin Luther King Jr. in Selma, and later served as special assistant to the president. In 1985, when I was appointed as Special Envoy to South Africa, Bob phoned me. Bob was chair of a railroad in North Carolina for which his great-grandfather had labored as a slave more than a hundred years earlier. Bob also had decades of business experience in Africa. He offered his assistance, believing he could do things through nongovernmental channels that might help advance our aims of fostering a peaceful postapartheid South Africa.

I accepted his generous offer, never imagining the central,

yet unrecognized role Bob would play in moving South Africa to a one-person, one-vote democracy. Bob was one of the few people granted permission to visit Nelson Mandela on Robben Island. Over time, great trust developed between the two men. Eventually that circle of trust expanded to President Botha of South Africa. Bob was a translator. He interpreted Mandela's thinking and intentions for President Botha and vice versa. What an important contribution at a vital moment in global events! Bob's selfless work helped move South Africa toward a true democratic, inclusive society. For my part, I was the grateful recipient of his selfless service.

The ancient country of Ethiopia has been important to me ever since I first landed in Addis Ababa as a twenty-four-year-old. I have sent many young people to spend time with my dear friend Abraham Fiseha and become involved with his unique work with young street kids. These Westerners always return with an entirely changed outlook, reevaluating their own lives and purpose. They go initially to give something to those less fortunate, and then they discover that the more they give, the more they receive in return. Their own first world problems seem relatively unimportant when viewed through the lens of Ethiopia's grinding poverty.

Our context can often shape how we see a problem. This is why travel is so important. When the context changes, what we understand to be a problem changes as well. Getting out of our small world to notice what others are facing is humbling and empowering.

When you give, do so from the heart. Don't worry about the dimensions of the gift, large or small, or whether it is in money or service. Sometimes the tiniest gestures have the most impact. Throughout life, I've attempted to share with others what Ethiopia has given to me. In many respects, that ancient land has shaped who I am.

When Barack Obama was elected to the US Senate in 2005, I had an unusual encounter with him. I was waiting for a cab midmorning with my youngest son, Kempe, at the Washington Hilton Hotel in downtown Washington. While we stood there, the newly minted junior senator from Illinois approached me. He knew my name and was apparently aware of my interest in East Africa. He urged that we meet and do something together in that region of the world.

I was surprised by his interest and wanted to do something to encourage this young well-spoken leader. I have given out scores of ancient crosses from Ethiopia to various people, from NIH director Francis Collins to the lead singer of the band The Fray. At that moment, I was compelled to also give the junior senator such a gift. I simply said, "Senator Obama, I grew up here in Washington. It is a seductive political environment, yet I sense that there is a bigger purpose for your life, one that transcends even politics. And to remind you of this larger plan, here's a small antique Coptic cross from Ethiopia. You might carry it in your pocket or place it on your desk as a reminder of your life purpose."

I lost touch with Obama until January 31, 2009, on the

occasion of the Alfalfa Club's annual dinner in Washington. The Alfalfa dinner is a unique bipartisan annual gathering that is a spoof on politics and yet attracts the very top political and corporate leaders in our nation. During a break, I found myself alone with the president. He was seated at the raised dais. I approached him and said, "Mr. President, you won't likely recall an encounter we had some years ago when you were a newly elected senator."

When I stopped speaking, he silently stared at me for twenty seconds or more. After this long awkward pause, he opened his extended fist, revealing the Coptic cross I had given him years ago. I was speechless. We never know what small gestures might mean.

The opposite of amassing and accumulating as an end is giving. Ancient teachings are clear on this point: "Whoever loses his life . . . will find it."[11] It is only in giving that we truly find fulfillment and peace. We are intrinsically made as human beings to give our lives and resources for the benefit of others.

World-class investor and philanthropist Ray Chambers and I were on his plane flying to have lunch with the founder of Domino's Pizza in Detroit. Ray had the audacious idea of buying the company and providing "at risk" young people with the opportunity to be equity owners. As we entered the elevator, Ray asked out loud: "Why do I love giving my time and resources like this?"

I told him simply that I thought we were made to give; it is intrinsically who we are. Givers are happier, find greater peace, and often discover that good things come from their efforts. You reap what you sow.

During the nineteenth century, on an otherwise quiet afternoon, a poor Scottish farmer named Fleming was laboring in his fields, when he heard an agonized cry coming from a nearby bog. Immediately, he shifted focus and charged toward the troubling sound. He found in the dark muck, mired to his waist, a terrified boy, screaming and struggling to free himself from his downward trajectory and most certain death. Fleming saved the boy from what would have been his demise.

Days later an elegant carriage pulled up to the Scotsman's sparse dwelling. Out stepped a proper nobleman anxious to meet the farmer. The gentleman quickly introduced himself as the father of the young boy whom Fleming had so heroically saved days earlier. Because of this act of sacrifice, he wanted to reward the farmer handsomely. Fleming, clearly embarrassed by the attention, refused the gesture. But the nobleman saw a young boy hiding in the shadow of his father and inquired whether this was the farmer's lad. He was indeed. The nobleman suggested a deal: he would provide Fleming's son with the same level of education that his own son would enjoy. This was an offer that Fleming could not refuse.

Fleming's son attended the best schools and eventually graduated from St. Mary's Medical School in London, excelling in all that he touched. He was eventually knighted by the queen as Sir Alexander Fleming, discoverer of penicillin. Amazingly, this very drug, penicillin, would once again save the life of the nobleman's son. The nobleman's name was Lord Randolph Churchill and his son was Winston, who would later become prime minister. If you give, it comes back to you in some way.

There is some debate about whether children can be taught to be generous and to care about others. An Israeli study of six hundred parents who said they valued kindness and compassion found that those people frequently failed to raise children who shared those values.[12] It would seem that more is caught than taught in this respect. Passing on the ethic of generosity is not about mere words, but about modeling generous behavior. A study by psychologist Karen Caplovitz Barrett and colleagues indicates that the only effective way to instill generosity in children is through their observation of genuine role models. Children must observe adults who themselves truly care.[13] So much for the résumé-packing good works that we force our teenagers to perform for college applications. If they are doing caring things only for their résumé, it is not sustainable over the long run.

As I've traveled around the world, there is little doubt that those who give their lives for others and see that as their central organizing principle have great meaning and purpose in their lives. Our culture prizes achievements that make us bloated and lonely. We prioritize things over deep, meaningful connections. Only when we see our life's purpose through the lens of service and caring are we truly fulfilled.

Many individuals, both past and present, come to mind when I think of people who are forgiving and generous toward others. One unlikely person who fits that bill is John Newton.

Raised by a harsh seafaring father in the mid-1700s, Newton was an angry and bitter young man. He often found himself locked in the brig of a sailing vessel for his insubordinate behavior. In his early twenties, this hardened, profane sailor and slave trader experienced a spiritual conversion after his sober assessment of a life of debauchery and ruin. Overwhelmed that one as lost as he could find a new path, Newton later in life penned these famous lines: "Amazing Grace, how sweet the sound, that saved a wretch like me. I once was lost but now am found, was blind but now I see." "Amazing Grace" is one of the most beloved hymns of all time. Written in 1772, it describes Newton's tortured life and new path.

Our themes of forgiveness and service can be seen interwoven in this one changed life. Newton moved from an experience of grace, to an understanding of forgiveness, and finally to a life of service for both the powerful and the powerless. Newton was ordained a priest in the Anglican Church and had parishes in Olney and London, where he was popular for his preaching and pastoral care, especially among the poor. His later work included efforts to abolish the slave trade, in which he had once been an active participant. Here in one life is a powerful testament to the transformational possibilities that can occur when we look clear-eyed at ourselves and determine to change, forgive ourselves, and give back.

And it is never too late to make amends. V. J. Periyakoil, a Stanford geriatrics and palliative-care doctor, discovered that during their final days countless patients regretted never taking the time to mend broken relationships. This led to the

Stanford Letter Project, which encouraged dying patients to write that final letter and let go of hurt and disappointment. It is often the most important letter they have ever written. Shirley Jones wrote, "To Harold: You have forgotten to repay some of the personal loans you obtained from us. We are wiping your account cleared."[14] It takes great courage to face the unresolved in our hearts, but it is necessary if we are to find freedom.

Authentic leaders understand their vulnerabilities. Pride is our Achilles' heel and is utterly destructive to a life hungering for meaning. Giving and receiving forgiveness require humility and yet offer the doorway to living a life for others, which is central to a life of purposeful living and fulfillment.

TAKE ACTION:
Learning to Forgive and Serve

**The metric by which God will assess my life isn't dollars
but the individual people whose lives I've touched.**
—CLAYTON CHRISTENSEN,
PROFESSOR, HARVARD BUSINESS SCHOOL

In your journal reflect on these questions and exercises:

• *Were your parents or caregivers forgiving people?*

• *Are you a forgiving person? Write down examples
of times you forgave someone. Describe how those
experiences have influenced you.*

- *Do you keep score of your grievances against others? How is that working?*

- *Have there been times when others have forgiven you? Describe those experiences.*

- *Are there some things you think should never be forgiven?*

- *List at least five times you have cared for or served others outside of your family. How have those experiences affected you?*

- *Are you able to give to others even when it is not reciprocated? Why or why not?*

Define Success and Failure for Yourself

You may encounter many defeats, but you must not be defeated. In fact, it may be necessary to encounter the defeats, so you can know who you are, what you can rise from, how you can still come out of it.

—MAYA ANGELOU, AMERICAN POET

Failure is part of the success equation.

—MARK CUBAN, ENTREPRENEUR

Nothing strikes closer to the heart of what we truly value and believe than do our views of success and failure. They reveal it all!

Our task is to define success and failure for ourselves and so avoid unconsciously being driven by someone else's definitions. So what is *success*? It can be difficult to get our minds around this elusive concept. Our thinking on this matter is deeply embedded in our subconscious mind, and at times it even surprises us. Many of us have a "number," or amount of money, that seems to represent either security, success, or personal validation. It isn't wrong to set a financial goal—but is it enough? What would success look like if we viewed it through a different lens, one that included other measures such as deepening friendships, reconciling with others, giving back, or learning to be better versions of ourselves through meditation and exercise?

As noted earlier, PathNorth's original purpose was to help often isolated CEOs and business owners "broaden their definitions of success." Although the accumulation of wealth is certainly a prime motivator for many, success needs to be understood far more broadly. Those who see money and prestige as the primary measures of success are rarely happy and content. Quite the contrary. Sadly, many successful people who single-mindedly pursue those goals find they just don't deliver where it matters most. The earlier stories of Nelund, Persson, and others are striking cases in point.

So what's missing in narrow definitions of success? When disconnected from meaning, success seen only as wealth accumulation is simply sterile and unsatisfying. As we have seen, the hallmark of a satisfying and well-lived life requires having and maintaining authentic bonds with others. Success should incorporate this larger purpose. It is not something we should put off till later. By the time we come to this realization, it is often too late, as evidenced by the sad story of the Morgan Stanley banker I met. It has been deeply heartening throughout my journey to gather leaders to explore this very foreign territory of the heart and honestly look at the false gods our society so highly prizes.

I once chaired a panel with three individuals born into iconic American families, household names that are widely identified with great success: DuPont, Tyson, and Huizinga. All three panelists voiced a common sentiment: "Rather than advantaging me, my family name and history were at times paralyzing, as I tried to make my own way." We may not face such overt expectations, but perhaps there are some implicit ones driving us as well—unconscious definitions of success we have absorbed that end up paralyzing us.

It takes real strength to resist those gale winds pushing us to certain destinations. Sober reflection and finding your grounding are perhaps the only ways to stake your claim to be truly you. What do you care about? What are your values—not your family's or the broader culture's, but your own? Is your life philosophy sufficient for the task of enabling you to resist such implicit messaging and to build a definition of success that will last your entire life?

The ancient Greeks had a very different idea of "success" than we do. For them, the "good life" was about living a meaningful life and contributing to the greater good. They knew intuitively what research confirms: "givers" are happier and more fulfilled, because they have a purpose beyond themselves. But what is that purpose?

Many leaders lack the tools, emotional intelligence, or courage to venture out into this messy emotional landscape. Spending time reflecting on a well-crafted question can create a pause, a moment to consider and recalibrate goals. At a recent PathNorth salon, hosted in the lovely San Francisco home of Mike and Holly Depatie, the question was posed: What would your children say is most important to you?

After some initial discomfort, an electric evening resulted when those assembled shared some rather raw feelings and even some tears. They developed a different kind of relationship with each other, one that was more real, more true, more connected. The experience prompted many to rethink their lives.

How would you answer that question? In the journey toward becoming a better and more transparent person, half the battle is becoming comfortable enough to explore life's big questions.

Often at the end of a gathering at which leaders have reflected on the big questions of their lives, we at PathNorth urge the participants to put pen to paper and craft a brief letter to themselves outlining their regrets and the changes they intend to make in the future. We collect these and then mail them individually to the participants a month later. The letter reminds them of an extraordinary moment when they touched on something truly important. After a time of major reflection "on the mountaintop," so to speak, is over, people have a tendency to push back the big questions as they reenter their day-to-day worlds. Receiving a written copy of their reflections and promises from that time refreshes their memory and allows them to reengage and consider where they are in relation to the changes they wished to make.

Questions have a way of worming themselves into our hearts and minds. They prompt us to respond and struggle to be honest with ourselves. Here are additional questions you might use to pause and reflect upon:

- What fosters hope in you?
- How would you like to be remembered?
- How do you think you can get "unstuck" from a particular situation or behavior in your life?
- What would you shout from the mountaintop?
- What is the biggest obstacle keeping you from your personal greatness?
- Do you experience the "imposter syndrome"? How so?
- Whose life seems purposeful to you?

Becoming comfortable with thoughtful introspection is critically important if we are to rethink and reimagine ingrained notions of success and failure. In examining ourselves, it helps if we understand what factors shape our views and beliefs, particularly about what really matters.

The Temptation of "More"

"Why do people perpetually create for themselves the conditions for their own dissatisfaction?" questions Michael Lewis in *The New New Thing*. In his book, Lewis attempts to understand the insatiable aspect of wealth accumulation. He uses billionaire and entrepreneur James Clark as an example of someone who could never seem to have enough.

Clark is the founder of Netscape. Clark, prior to being worth billions, always believed that he'd be satisfied if he had just a bit more. His first goal was $10 million, but the number kept increasing. Every time he reached his goal, there was a higher number to strive for. At one point, Lewis reminded Clark that he had once told Lewis that when he became a real after-tax billionaire, he'd retire and be satisfied.

Clark swiftly retorted, "I just want to make more money than Larry Ellison. Then I'll stop."

Lewis then asked him if he wanted to surpass the wealth of Bill Gates.

Clark replied, emphatically, "No, that'll never happen."

After a few minutes, Clark self-corrected. "You know," he said, "just for one moment, I would kind of like to have the most, just for one tiny moment."[1]

Although it's easy to judge, Clark's behavior isn't that unusual. It's a human tendency to never be satisfied. How much is enough? Just a little bit more.

Our insecurities and demons can make us feel as though we never have enough or that we ourselves are not enough. Most of us realize on some level that we are chasing a fantasy, that illusive "more." We might even try to shift the narrative, justifying our hungry pursuit as something we're doing for our families or employees rather than ourselves. Yet there is a deep hole inside where our restlessness and emptiness reside.

Pascal described this as an existential hole in the heart of every human. He called it a "God-shaped vacuum." He saw the ache as part of our human condition, a longing for the numinous, not just the material. But the illusive "more" on the material level merely transports us farther from our heart's desire. Research shows that after hitting the benchmark of $75,000 annually, one's happiness does not increase with more money.[2]

The fables and moral tales of Leo Tolstoy have much to teach us about the dark side of success. In the short story "How Much Land Does a Man Need?" Tolstoy writes about a young ambitious Russian farmer named Pahom, who seeks to expand his farming enterprise by traveling eastward to the land of the nomadic Bashkir tribe. Pahom tries to buy land but is rebuffed and instead presented with a novel way to achieve his goal. The Bashkirs were willing to give him as much land as he could circumscribe on foot between sunup and sundown.

It seemed too good to be true! Still, Pahom sets off early the next morning, filled with raging ambition. As Pahom walks, he quickens his pace and delights in the beauty and vitality of the land. He charts a large course, pushing himself to the limit, all the while keeping a watchful eye on the sun. He's utterly exhausted by sunset but successful. He has completed the enormous loop securing unimaginable wealth.

As the sun sinks below the horizon, he falls prostrate and utterly spent at the feet of the Bashkir chief. The Bashkirs cheer wildly for this incredible achievement. But Pahom doesn't rise in celebration. He lies dead from the very pursuit of his prize. Tolstoy concludes with the haunting line: "His servant picked up the spade and dug a grave long enough for Pahom to lie in and buried him in it. Six feet from his head to his heels was all he needed."

Ka-boom! How often do we reach for a goal without considering the cost of achieving it? What should we be seeking? When we avoid these questions, we run the risk of becoming as hollow as the object of our affections.

As I walk around Washington or New York, I frequently spot individuals who used to "be somebody." Success and notoriety are fleeting. Former senator Richard Lugar had offices in our building. Lugar was a friend and a giant in so many ways. He was a Rhodes scholar and mayor of Indianapolis; he served six terms in the US Senate and was chair of the powerful Foreign Relations Committee. Yet few recognized him as he walked Washington's streets today.

Few accomplished individuals think that at some point they will be an afterthought, a mere footnote in history—but such is life. As one retired CEO told me, "I went from 'Who's Who' to 'Who's that?'" We pursue success in all of its shapes and colors. We amass wealth and toys. And we do it all as though we will be feted forever.

In his fascinating book *Die Broke*, author Stephen Pollan, a Manhattan financial planner, observed a puzzling phenomenon among his wealthiest clients. No matter how wealthy his clients were, they never felt secure or successful enough. Pollan came to a startling conclusion. Simply put, his clients refused to believe that they would ever die. They were building and accumulating as though they'd live forever.[3]

So Pollan urged his clients to pick an age when they thought they might die. He urged them to live with that limited horizon in mind. If you only have twenty years to live, why not use your resources to improve the lives of those you love? Invest in memorable experiences for your family. Buy meaningful gifts for those who have meant much to you over your lifetime. Pollan found a way to help his clients reimagine their futures. Rather than chasing empty goals, they shifted to a much richer narrative. Success will end sadly if it is decoupled from our humanity. It's essential to nurture our relationships and underscore our core values in order to live a fulfilling life.

The Importance of Failure

A fascinating study by Boston College researcher Karen Arnold followed eighty-one high-school valedictorians and salutatorians from graduation onward. The goal was to determine how those achievers fared in life, given their impeccable pedigrees. Certainly, they were all highly accomplished and reliable. Yet how many of these superperformers went on to change the world?

The answer was, surprisingly, zero. The research revealed that impressive traits in the classroom, in fact, disqualify an overachieving student from having a significant impact in later life. As Arnold says, "Valedictorians aren't likely to be the future's visionaries. . . . They typically settle into the system instead of shaking it up." Schools celebrate students who do what they are told. Arnold concludes, "Essentially, we are rewarding conformity and the willingness to go along with the system."[4]

Following the rules can protect you against failure, but it won't lead to innovation. What if success were more broadly understood as something that intrinsically included failure in its very design? Failure is a critical part of the journey if your goal is to push conventional boundaries and hope for real impact.

We're taught to downplay or even hide our failures and embellish our accomplishments. But what do we lose if we follow that rule? Princeton professor Johannes Haushofer decided to prepare a résumé of his illustrious failures. He called it the Curriculum Vitae of Failures and posted it on Twitter for the world to see. Haushofer noted, "Most of what I try fails, but these failures are often invisible, while the successes are visible. I have noticed that this sometimes gives others the impression that most things work out for me." In his opinion, projecting only success has a highly damaging effect. His post got a lot of attention, prompting Haushofer to observe, tongue-in-cheek, "This darn CV of Failures has received way more attention than my entire body of academic work."[5] Yet such authenticity is indeed attractive. He exposed the truth: the path to success is riddled with failure along the way. We all know this, and yet few are brave enough to speak it out loud.

Paradoxically, failures can set us on a path to real success. Setbacks can actually mark a new beginning if we heed their lessons. It's just a matter of taking the time to reflect during teachable moments. When you are tested in some way—a health problem, divorce, loss of a child, being fired—you can emerge with a deeper resolve and even less fear. It all rests on how you think. As Solomon voiced, "For as [a man] thinks in his heart, so is he."[6]

A failure can feel like a setback, but it can also provide fuel for moving forward. Rejection should not have the final word. The first children's book by Dr. Seuss (Theodor Seuss Geisel), *And to Think That I Saw It on Mulberry Street*, was rejected by twenty-seven publishers. Dr. Seuss didn't give up. The twenty-eighth publisher he reached out to, Vanguard Press, accepted the book. This debut went on to sell six million copies. The great influencers over time didn't escape rejection. They worked through it.

David Hartman was blind at age eight, but, as a young adult, he was determined to become a doctor. At the time, the early 1970s, no blind person had ever completed medical school. Hartman was rejected by nine medical schools. He persisted and finally, at age twenty-six, graduated from Temple University in Philadelphia, a doctor. General Douglas MacArthur was denied admission to West Point not once, but twice. If you're passionate about something, you can't let others determine your destiny. The German philosopher Friedrich Nietzsche gave voice to such resilience: "That which does not kill me makes me stronger."

If you feel like a failure, try connecting with someone worse off than you. One morning during a business breakfast in New York, a hedge-fund manager had a question for Harvard psychiatrist Armand Nicholi. Nicholi and I had been working on a PBS film documentary that was contrasting the philosophic worldviews of Sigmund Freud and C. S. Lewis. He asked Nicholi, "If an individual was in extremis across the street, ready to end his life, and you had only one intervention to alter his course, what would you do?"

Nicholi initially refused to answer the hypothetical question, but the hedge-fund manager persisted. Finally, Nicholi offered a response. He said, "I would urge the troubled man to get involved with and help someone worse off than himself." He went on to explain that it can be truly transformational to be a giver and can even change your body chemistry as well as emotional outlook. So despite your personal state of mind, it always helps to lean forward and give.

The binary notion of success and failure is a flawed construct. The world does not operate in black and white. In the film *Charlie Wilson's War*, an ancient story is told about what is good and what is bad. In the story, a farmer has only one horse, and one day it runs away. The neighbors console the farmer over his terrible loss. "Such bad luck!" they cry. The farmer shrugs. He says, "Who knows what is bad and what is good?"

A month later, the horse returns, bringing with him two wild horses. Excited, the neighbors say, "Good luck, indeed!" Again, the farmer shrugs and says, "Who knows what is bad and what is good?"

Shortly after, the farmer's son is thrown from one of the wild horses and breaks his leg. Bad luck, according to the neighbors. Again the farmer says, "Who knows what is bad and what is good?"

Next, a tribal battle ensues. Every able-bodied man is sent into battle. The farmer's son stays behind because of his leg. The neighbors congratulate the farmer, who again murmurs, "Who knows what is bad and what is good?"

Our perspective on a problem is the factor that decides how that problem will impact our lives. Setbacks can mark a new beginning if only we pay attention. Pain is God's "megaphone," observed C. S. Lewis. Pain can stop us cold. It forces us to take stock, consider possibilities, and adjust to a new reality.

Dan Ariely, a Duke University behavioral economist, came to his profession after a tragic event. He was badly burned when a flare accidentally exploded, leaving him with third-degree burns over 70 percent of his body. Instead of sending this young man's life careening off course, it produced the opposite result. During his slow and painful recovery, Ariely began to "notice and record things." According to him, he had little else to do in the hospital ward. This newfound curiosity inspired Ariely to study human behavior. His research in the area of resilience is particularly groundbreaking, and it was born out of a seeming tragedy.

In our metrics-oriented culture, where everything is a test to pass, failure teaches us a different kind of lesson. J. K. Rowling, author of the Harry Potter series, gave a commencement speech at Harvard University several years ago.

It is one of the most riveting speeches I've ever heard. She mentioned her life of poverty before fame, but then declared, "What I feared most for myself at your age was not poverty, but failure." She was well aware of her privileged, high-achieving audience. She noted, "The fact that you are graduating from Harvard suggests that you are not very well-acquainted with failure. You might be driven by a fear of failure quite as much as a desire for success." Rowling said she values failure. For her, "Failure meant a stripping away of the inessential. I stopped pretending to myself that I was anything other than what I was. . . . And so rock bottom became the solid foundation on which I rebuilt my life."[7]

If we're too afraid to fail, then we miss out on the kind of critical self-evaluation that, for Rowling, was foundational. Mike West, an entrepreneur from Knoxville, always unsettles my MBA class when he urges them to embrace failure quickly. Oddly enough, failure produces an inner security that can be attained in no other way. Failure makes us stronger and wiser. After all, life is 10 percent what actually happens to us and 90 percent how we respond.

We would never choose to be faced with a serious problem that rocks our world, but a setback can be an opportunity to redefine the way we approach life. After a difficult medical diagnosis, Harvard Business School professor Clayton Christensen reevaluated the impact of his life. He noted, "This past year I was diagnosed with cancer and faced the possibility that my life would end sooner than I'd planned. . . . I have a pretty clear idea of how my ideas have generated enormous revenue for companies that have used my research; I know I've had a substantial impact. But as I've confronted this disease, it's been interesting to see how unimportant that impact is to me now."[8]

In the face of a major setback, Christensen was able to clear the brush and reframe a new paradigm for his life. We all have to deal with unexpected blows. No one is immune. As Jesus wisely predicted, "In this world, you will have trouble."[9] So embrace changed circumstances after you've had a good cry. Allow that new reality to do its refining and clarifying work in your life.

Could it be that the very things we dread—setback and failure—truly are the teachers for a life of meaning and thriving? Do they help us embark on a pathway to real success?

Failure is actually central to success. Just ask Babe Ruth. Yes, he held the major league home-run record, and yet he also held the strike-out record. Or consider Thomas Edison. He held over one thousand patents. He invented the lightbulb and the phonograph, among many other innovations. However, he failed with such novelties as the electric pen. His perspective on failure was instructive. He observed, "I have not failed ten thousand times. I've successfully found ten thousand ways that will not work."

Perhaps the things you once considered your greatest failings might become the shapers of a better, deeper you. Basing our self-worth on the flawed notion that our identity is only tied to our professional accomplishments and "wins" is wrongheaded and highly destructive. Authentic people view failure not as the end, but as the beginning of a journey of discovery grounded in humility.

Thrive with Resilience

As we develop our own definition of success, one that makes room for failure, a necessary trait becomes obvious: *resilience*. If we do not know how to bounce back from failure or hardship, then we may never achieve the success we seek.

Research is clear that those who thrive are resilient. Success seldom comes to people who live problem-free. Setback and adversity can provide opportunities to test and develop your resilience. My friend and investment partner Bill Mayer has observed that the best way to see if someone is a great leader is to place them in a circumstance where they need to "figure it out" for themselves. He divides people into two categories: the ones who, if stranded on a remote island, would quickly die, and the others, who would find a way to survive. Which are you?

I've long pondered the relationship between suffering or setback and resilience. The French existentialist Albert Camus observed a powerful connection between these forces in himself. He declared, "In the midst of winter, I finally found there was, within me, an invincible summer." Camus is pointing to a moment of discovery of inner strength that had been unacknowledged up to that point.

I've wondered whether people are born with resilience or is it a learned behavior. According to UCLA Health, "Resiliency is a cultivated habit. The more you practice it, the greater your ability to bounce back from adversity. It's not about pretending everything is fine. Rather, it's about developing healthy life management skills."[10]

I tend to agree. Clearly, some are born with a more sunny, resilient outlook, but resilience can be built and strengthened through positive attitudes and practices. You can learn and improve resiliency skills every day. Don't wait for trying times to test your resilience. Create a solid foundation, one that will enable you to weather those severe times. Be a communicator with yourself and others. Meditate, converse, and reframe situations. Focus on gratitude and laughing. All of these actions decrease stress hormones and boost the immune system, making you stronger and more resilient.

The American Psychological Association defines resilience as "adapting well in the face of adversity, trauma, tragedy, threats, or significant sources of stress." In its opinion, rather than viewing resilience as a one-time occurrence when you have to "bounce back," we should think of it as an ongoing practice.[11] In other words, as we do in learning any new skill, we need to *practice* resilience.

In 1962, psychologists Victor and Mildred Goertzel published *Cradles of Eminence: A Provocative Study of the*

Childhoods of Over 400 Famous Twentieth-Century Men and Women. Despite its catchy title, the book is loaded with useful data. The Goertzels focused on famous people who had positively impacted society, from Henry Ford and Eleanor Roosevelt to Marie Curie and Louis Armstrong. Shockingly, the Goertzels discovered that only 15 percent of their subjects were raised in stable, supportive homes. Of the four hundred, 75 percent, or three hundred people, grew up in environments with severe problems, such as abuse, alcoholism, abandonment, or some other misfortune. The authors concluded, "The 'normal' man is not a likely candidate for the Hall of Fame."[12]

Today's list would include LeBron James, Howard Schultz, and Oprah Winfrey, among others. These people share a common trait—determination, or an inner defiance—that has played an important role in their success. They have all mastered the art of resilience, of not letting others define their path. One military officer described how he survived years of bullying as a child: "I refused to accept that what they said about me was true."

I once heard of two brothers raised in a home with a violent alcoholic father. One brother grew up to be a model citizen and a good abstinent parent, while the other became a hopeless drunk, prone to abuse. When asked how they came to be who they were, both answered, "Given who my father was, how could I not?" We all have the opportunity to shape our stories, even when we are told otherwise. We have choices.

Poet Dylan Thomas wrote, "There's only one thing that's

worse than having an unhappy childhood, and that's having a too-happy childhood." Adversity might not catapult everyone to fame, but to a large extent it can help us become more resilient and appreciative. In a multiyear study of adults aged 18 to 101 at the University of Buffalo, psychologist Mark Seery found that subjects who had known some type of adversity were higher functioning and more satisfied than others.[13] This is a surprising and yet hopeful truth. Adversity frequently sets us on a positive course.

There are many ways to endure adversity: we may tackle a situation head-on or take a more subtle approach. Our state of being before being faced with a setback will define how we navigate it. Kelly McGonigal, a health psychologist at Stanford, presented interesting information about mortality in a 2013 TED Talk. According to McGonigal, major stressful experiences, such as a personal financial crisis or divorce, increase our risk of dying by 30 percent. However, she also shared that those who spent their days caring for others showed absolutely no stress-related increased risk in dying. Zero.[14] So the deadly effects of stress are not inevitable and can be managed through practices of selfless caring. We find here that reaching out to others in need enhances resilience.

Resilience is, at its core, an interior strength. In his short work *Man's Search for Meaning*, Viktor Frankl notes that those who survived the Nazi death camps were not the physically robust, but rather those with a rich interior life of the mind and spirit. Often they had a purpose for wanting to survive, such as to see a grandchild play the violin again, and so on. Once, when I was speaking with a couple of Navy Seals who endured the arduous training regimen known as BUD/S School, they told me that much more important than athletic and physical prowess was a fierce interior resolve. I'm not surprised.

You can begin to develop resilience at any point in life. Once you begin your work life, it's a process of constant discovery. M. Scott Peck begins his classic work *The Road Less Traveled* with this line: "Life is difficult."[15] It's true. Life is wrought with twists and turns. It is a difficult odyssey. A 2016 Brookings Institute study of the relationship between age and happiness found that the low point of happiness was between the ages of twenty-five and forty-seven, with the lowest point at around age forty.[16] Such conclusions are hardly reassuring to college graduates. But perhaps it also means that, over time, we begin to become more comfortable with how unpredictable life is and thus more resilient and accepting. Simply showing up, even when you don't feel like it, produces a strength.

Obstacles are there for us to surmount and for our growth. Adversity and suffering are useful in sculpting a life. Only adversity can remind us about what matters most. It prepares us to appreciate the range of life experiences and what each can teach us. So how are we to think about suffering, pain, and hardship? I would suggest that we summon our inner fighter and take the long view. However you were shaped growing up, you have the power of choice on your side. You can choose a different path. If we view setbacks, failures, and adversity as opportunities, then we set ourselves up to succeed and grow.

Basketball icon Michael Jordan described it best: "I've missed more than nine thousand shots in my career. I've lost almost three hundred games. Twenty-six times I've been trusted to take the game-winning shot and missed. I've failed over and over and over again in my life. And that is why I succeed." Your turn . . .

TAKE ACTION:
Determining Your Definitions of Success and Failure

You can get all As and still flunk life.
—**WALKER PERCY, AUTHOR**

In your journal reflect on these questions and exercises:

- *How did your family define success? How was this celebrated?*

- *What messages from the broader culture have you received regarding success? How has this influenced your view?*

- *How do you define success? Are you a success?*

- *Do you have a specific measure for success? How much is enough?*

- *When did you fail? What did you feel afterward? What did you learn from it?*

- *Describe two experiences you have had in which you have shown resilience. What motivated you to persevere in these situations?*

- *What would your children say is most important to you? What would you like them to say?*

———————————————————————

— 7 —

Invite Risk into Your Life

The greatest danger for most of us is not
that our aim is too high and we miss it,
but that it is too low and we reach it.
—MICHELANGELO

I knew that if I failed, I wouldn't regret that, but I
knew the one thing I might regret is not trying.
—JEFF BEZOS, FOUNDER OF AMAZON

Many of us grew up believing that risk was a bad thing. It evoked a sense of recklessness and irresponsibility. Perhaps you had a relative like my uncle Jack, who seemed to conceive an endless number of business ideas and yet none materialized. (In truth, he had perhaps a little too much fondness for the bottle!) At the other end of the spectrum was my accountant father, a real steady Eddie who worked for the same organization for forty-two years. His routine was consistent to a fault, always the same, stable and reliable. In this respect and for those times, he was a virtuous model.

Today, the paradigm has shifted. Young entrepreneurs are breaking rules and boundaries. They are casting caution to the wind. This approach to risk-taking, making daring choices to create the next "new" thing, is now prized above all else. So which is it? Is risk good or worrisome? And if risk is to be valued and welcomed because it is elemental to a life of meaning, how does one become a prudent risk-taker? Is the ability innate or nurtured?

As in other important matters, our view of risk was shaped by the practices we observed early on. We either embraced what we saw in our homes in those formative years or reacted against those very practices.

Margot Bisnow, who studies entrepreneurship, has long puzzled over the notion of risk-taking. She shed some light on the subject for me from a unique vantage point by asking the question, "What makes an entrepreneur comfortable with risk?" Bisnow took a straightforward tack to discover the answer to this question. She asked young entrepreneurs if their parents raised them to be this way. Their answers were surprisingly consistent. These young entrepreneurial risk-takers all had a parent or caregiver who believed in them, period.[1]

Being an entrepreneur is bruising and hard, full of self-doubt and fearfulness. Inevitably, your mind is swimming with voices, internal and external, urging you to give up, grow up, and get a "normal" job. You need that one reassuring voice that believes in you, often when you don't see the way forward.

As to whether all young people, entrepreneurs or not, should embrace risk, Bisnow observes, "Raising a child to be proud of his skills, to be confident, to be fearless, and to have a strong work ethic seems to me like a fine approach with any child." Strong emotional support might produce a gifted college dropout who launches an internet company, a steady professional who earns a law degree and practices that craft dutifully, or even a fifth-grade teacher who relishes shaping young minds. The path taken is almost immaterial. The main thing is that we're able to face our fears and simply do it, whether we embark on what is perceived as high-risk or not.

I have found that if our goal is to live risk-free, we will not end up living meaningful, fulfilling, and successful lives. Without risk, we do not grow. We do not all need to be extreme or even entrepreneurial risk-takers, but we all need to learn to value and exercise some risk-taking in our lives.

Know Your Personal Risk Tolerance

The fact is, life is risky for everyone, and yet our personal estimation of what constitutes a risk is relative and cannot be compared with others. What is high-risk for one person is not necessarily considered risky for another. We all need to understand our personal risk tolerance. It doesn't help to

compare ourselves to others. As we move forward in any en-
deavor, we must face our own fears and launch out. We simply
can't sail to any new destination while moored to the dock.
Our fears tether us to that stable dock, which, though initially
comfortable and familiar, over time causes us to live a fear-
based defensive existence.

So whatever your risk profile, risks present themselves for
our personal growth. As a friend recently said to me, "Walls
and obstacles are there for a reason, for us to consider how
badly we want it and what we are willing to do to overcome
the barriers."

David Dobbs, of *National Geographic*, describes our innate
need to explore: "The compulsion to see what lies beyond that
far ridge or that ocean—or this planet—is a defining part of
human identity and success."[2] Risk isn't just for *National Geographic* explorers or untethered wild people; all of us need to
venture out, in one way or another. It is intrinsic to being human. To thrive entails that we grow, and in order to grow we
will encounter risk.

But aren't there unhealthy risks and practices to avoid?
Certainly. Michael Kennedy, son of the late Robert Kennedy,
spent a day with me in New York some years ago. The occasion
that brought us together was not great. His cousin asked
that I talk with him about the travails he was enduring. I was
struck by Michael's intelligence, but also by his appetite for
risk-taking.

Michael joined me at a breakfast discussion the next morning where Ralph Larsen, then chair and CEO of Johnson & Johnson, led a conversation on the subject of death. Impulsively, I turned to Michael and asked him a blunt question. As the words tumbled from my mouth, I wondered how I could be so insensitive: "So, Michael, how do you make sense of death, particularly in light of the tragic assassinations of both your uncle, JFK, and your dear father, Bobby Kennedy?"

But Michael didn't miss a beat. He first said that his family was well acquainted with death and grief; it was a regular occurrence in their large family. He then added that his family was almost philosophical rather than emotional about death and the risky decisions that the Kennedys had a habit of making. His response was unexpected but understandable when you consider all of the Kennedy tragedies—what one writer dubbed the "Kennedy curse." And the sad saga continued. Following that breakfast, Michael took off for Aspen with several of his cousins for some skiing. The cousins were tossing a football back and forth as they barreled down a steep ski slope. Michael hit a tree and instantly died.

I was stunned and saddened by this tragic turn of events. Later I reflected upon our private conversations and wondered what possessed Michael to push the limits so far. I became more and more curious about the notion of risk-taking, both the wondrous side, which has led to great innovation, and the darker side, which can lead into dangerous waters, often with dire outcomes.

Avoiding risk has its own set of challenges. This is an angle we tend not to consider. Years ago, Glenn Youngkin was in charge of European operations for the Carlyle Group, a large private-equity firm, where he is now CEO. Glenn had it all: he was a former college athlete, tall and handsome; a Baker scholar at the Harvard Business School; and successful with his company's investment portfolio. Glenn was excited when he was summoned back to Washington to meet with one of the founding partners. It always feels good to be affirmed for stellar work. So imagine his shock, when, while sitting on the back porch of the founder's stunning Virginia home, Glenn was told that perhaps he should look for another job.

He was astonished. Why? This made no sense. His numbers were superb!

The founders had concluded that Glenn was just too risk-averse. He was not venturing out and taking appropriate risks to seize new opportunities. This conversation changed Glenn's life. He hit pause and conducted a life inventory. He soon concluded that, indeed, not only was he doing business defensively, but he was living defensively in his personal life as well.

After a period of soul searching, Glenn made an important shift that affected a number of important areas of his life. It was time to embrace greater risk and inculcate this mindset into various aspects of both his business and personal practices. It took time to create and follow new patterns, but it came to pass. He is now a better business leader and, more important, a better person. You'll never win any game if you are playing just to avoid injury. The purpose is to win, and that typically involves risk.

There are many approaches to risk-taking, from reckless to wise. Knowing what to do when requires practice and introspection.

Take Good Risks

I was surprised to learn that about 20 percent of people possess a mutated gene that causes them to be more curious than others and to assume greater risks. This gene is called *DRD4-7R*. It triggers restlessness and an appetite to explore new ideas, people, experiences, food, and more. One researcher observed that historically individuals who possessed the "explorer's gene" but lived risk-adverse, settled village existences tended to "wither" and become malnourished. And conversely, when these similar individuals allowed their unique wiring to spur them to venture out and explore, they thrived.[3]

It is critical to create an environment that enables us to take appropriate risks. That environment isn't just a place; it's a mindset. Children who are encouraged to play and explore are more comfortable with risk and its range of implications.

Unfortunately, parents' need for control and their expectations can put the screws to that. Often at airports I observe overwhelmed "responsible" parents scolding their young,

restless children. "Johnny, stop running. Sit down and behave," they chide, when all their children were doing was en-
ergetically exploring their new environment. The desire for
control and order can stifle the imaginative, risk-taking side
of a young person. Too frequently, we project our fears onto
our children. They must be allowed to push frontiers, make
mistakes, and discover new paths.

We are made to explore. As we get older, social cues become more pronounced. Alison Gopnik, child-development
psychologist at UC–Berkeley, observes, "We do less [play] as
we get older . . . and become less willing to explore novel
alternatives and more conditioned to stick with familiar
ones."[4] We'd all be better off if we ignored certain social cues
and embraced that inherent love of risk and play from our
youth.

We need to rediscover and delight in risk. It will enliven
us and engender a sense of confidence and wonder. Become
childlike again. Push beyond your comfort zone in small
ways. It is energizing.

On YouTube you can watch Floridian Bernice Bates, who
is in her midnineties and once held the Guinness World Record for being the oldest yoga instructor.[5] She began practicing yoga over fifty years ago, and it's obviously working for
her. Bernice has no health problems and takes no medication.
She is an avid gardener, lifts weights, attends church, swims,
and talks smack about her beloved Tampa Bay Rays. She also
learned ballroom dancing in her late eighties and dances with

her much younger male dance partner. Talk about risk! When you see her dance, it is hard not to be inspired and motivated. She simply keeps growing and expanding her notion of the possible. She is delighting in life and eager to discover what awaits. What a rich existence, full of discovery and forward thinking.

Whether you have the risk gene or not, the value of good risk-taking is unmistakable. Research supports that some amount of discomfort is involved in attaining true happiness. Often we must do things that are initially uncomfortable and unfamiliar and yet later become associated with some of our finest moments. Psychologists Robert Biswas-Diener and Todd Kashdan note: "Truly happy people seem to have an intuitive grasp of the fact that sustained happiness is not just about doing things that you like. It also requires growth and adventuring beyond the boundaries of your comfort zone."[6]

This doesn't necessarily mean we must take a big ugly leap of some sort. We can develop a habit of risk-taking in small ways. We then taste the benefits and expand our scope of activity. Try a new restaurant. Have a conversation with someone you wouldn't typically reach out to, like an old or estranged friend. Read a book outside of your usual genre. Meditate for ten minutes. Learn a language. Ask a monk about his "calling." By starting small, you'll start to see that risk, the unfamiliar, is your friend and teacher.

Social commentator Studs Terkel interviewed individuals over the age of ninety about their regrets. One of their top two regrets was not having taken enough risks. They felt they missed out on some great experiences by simply playing it too safe.[7]

We experience a range of emotions when we embrace a risk and chart a new direction. My oldest son, Ry, sent me a quote from the Hindu teacher Nisargadatta Maharaj that reflects this internal struggle: "There are always moments when one feels empty and estranged. Such moments are most desirable, for it means the soul has cast its moorings and is sailing for distant places . . . when the old is over and the new has not yet come. If you are afraid, the state may be distressing, but there is really nothing to be afraid of."

The Danish philosopher Søren Kierkegaard described the "knight of faith" as one who, in faith, ventures out to a new land to face and conquer whatever awaits. And yes, it is fearful, yet deeply satisfying, and it reinforces itself when regularly repeated.

For me, Jesus is a fascinating historical figure. He spoke in parables, which were designed to reveal important truths to those who were ready to hear them, while concealing his insights from those not prepared for the implications of such daring and highly irregular teaching. His parable about the talents is an interesting study of risk.[8]

A talent was a fairly large monetary unit in biblical times. As Jesus tells the story, a business owner was going abroad for a period of time, so he called three of his servants and entrusted them with various amounts of money. To one he gave five talents; to the second, two talents; and to the last, one. Upon his return, he summoned the three to account for their stewardship of his investment. The servants with five and two talents had invested the money and doubled it. The last servant had only the one original talent in hand, with no increase. The owner was outraged. He cast the last servant out.

As an investor, I long puzzled over this parable. It is not a terrible thing to refrain from investing, to stay liquid and hold on to your principal, during uncertain markets. Additionally, a parable was intended to offer a glimpse into the very character of God. The business owner's behavior is hardly a flattering portrait of the Almighty. Why would God be so upset over the third servant's careful and prudent approach to investing his master's valued property?

Then the light came on! The servant told the business owner that he was too afraid to even deposit the money in a bank. Instead, he buried it in the ground. Fear was the issue. The master's anger was not about ROI (return on investment). He was furious that his servant had been paralyzed by his fear and that fear caused him to fail to act decisively and boldly. In fact, I believe that if the servant had invested that one talent in a failed biotech company, the master would have celebrated a calculated risk even if it did not work out.

Wharton professor Adam Grant argues that companies with strong cultures, although appealing on one level, have unintended perils as well. Such businesses certainly attract motivated and talented people. But, as the culture grows, it becomes more entrenched. The business then trends toward inertia and stagnation, with little place for innovation and risk-taking. An overwhelmingly strong business culture can crowd out diversity of thought and imaginative risk-taking. The net result is that such companies cease to grow and flourish as in earlier days. There is simply too much to lose.[9]

Sometimes when we trust our instincts and take risks, surprising results occur. When I served on the White House staff, bipartisanship and compromise were considered good things, so it wasn't unusual to connect across party lines. In 1985, Florida senator Bill Nelson, a Democrat and then congressman, and I took a private cargo plane loaded with bags of grain to northern Ethiopia. Ethiopia was experiencing one of the most severe famines in modern times. Hundreds of thousands of people were dying. The Marxist government publicly denied that the famine even existed; meanwhile, it was confiscating foreign-aid supplies and selling them on the black market instead of using them to feed its starving. This trip was risky, but it was the right thing to do.

We wanted to deliver food directly to trusted nongovernmental agencies to ensure that it didn't end up in the wrong hands on the black market. We flew directly for nineteen hours and slept on top of large grain bags, since all seating had been removed to make room for our precious cargo. When we finally arrived, we observed hundreds of thousands of Ethiopians as far as the eye could see, waiting in a large expanse of parched ground, silently hoping for food to avert imminent starvation. It was still, so still across that large dry expanse. The people waiting were simply too weak to even cry. It was very eerie, an experience I will never forget.

After those brown burlap bags had been unloaded into the safe hands of the courageous relief workers, I turned to Congressman Nelson with another crazy idea. "Bill," I said, "since we are here, let's fly down to the capital, Addis Ababa, to meet with the foreign minister to talk about this dire situation. Let's just do it!" With little thought, we were off for Addis Ababa.

We met with the Ethiopian leader for several hours. As the time passed, we listened to him lecture us endlessly on the merits of Marxist dialectical materialism. What fun! No—ridiculous. Finally, I had had enough. I took off my gold Ethiopian ring with the seal of the lion of Judah on its face. I had acquired the ring on my very first visit to Ethiopia a decade earlier. I asked the foreign minister to look at the ring and to tell me how the national symbol had been altered by his Marxist colleagues. He paused, examined my ring, and explained how his government had removed the cross on the head of the lion, since any view of God or the transcendent was incompatible with the governing ideology.

I told him my opinion was that this decision was at the heart of Ethiopia's dysfunction and heartache. He paused and pushed back slightly. Then the meeting concluded.

Yet barely two weeks later in Washington I received a call from the State Department. The foreign minister had defected and was en route to the United States. Our conversation had an impact. The trip had certainly been worth the risk and discomfort. Sometimes just showing up and moving into unfamiliar places can change everything. As Woody Allen once suggested, "Most of life is just showing up." How true.

Religious faith can hold important lessons about risk. Given some of the images we have in our minds about God and faith—for example, God as a celestial Santa Claus, jolly and irrelevant—it's understandable that we wouldn't immediately equate faith with risk-taking. Yet that is exactly what it is. Faith is another way of knowing. It is not blind, but rather is an extension of our other senses. Philosophers and theologians call this area of study epistemology, how we know what we know. Faith involves risk, because what we believe in can't be perceived by our five senses alone. It is another way of "knowing."

Risk-taking in faith isn't necessarily safe. It can, in fact, feel dangerous and unsettling. At times it compels us to venture into unknown places. C. S. Lewis wrote a series of books, The Chronicles of Narnia, to tell stories about the journey of faith through a child-friendly lens, but also so that adults might understand his keen insights. You might recall that the powerful lion, Aslan, was the archetype for God. He was a ferocious force for good and against evil. When Lucy was attempting to understand what Aslan was truly like, she asked the beavers if he was safe.

"Safe?" said Mr. Beaver. "Don't you hear what Mrs. Beaver

tells you? Who said anything about safe? 'Course he isn't safe. But he's good. He's the King, I tell you."

I believe that God is dangerous, in a good sense. If we enter into a partnership with him, where risk is central, he will take us to unimaginable places to do unimaginable things. It's a risk to be a follower. Ask the disciples of Jesus, who all met their end by following a dangerous God. Most believers would say that God is good and well worth the risk.

Success isn't guaranteed if you take bold action. However, you won't get anywhere if you aren't willing to break away from comfortable routines and established norms, to be imaginative, and to venture something different. My sister Sandra is a syndicated columnist and the premier pattern designer for *Vogue Patterns*. One day she saw an opportunity. Celebrated Japanese designer Issey Miyake was coming to San Francisco to unveil his collection. Miyake rarely grants interviews. Sandra wanted one, and to secure a prized interview, she needed to get his attention. Then an idea struck requiring a bold move on her part.

She'd had a sneak preview from *Vogue* of his upcoming collection. She made an exact copy of one of his signature dresses and wore it to the fashion show in Miyake's honor. When she entered the room, Miyake looked astonished. He made a beeline for the beautiful woman in his lovely frock. They talked and talked. He invited her to visit him in Tokyo, where she interviewed him for *Threads* magazine. Sandra embraced the unknown and took a chance. Her risk paid off.

One of my favorite people is Jean Case, CEO of the Case Foundation, an organization designed to bring innovative and imaginative thinking to complex social problems. When considering the fifteen-year milestone of this unique and rule-breaking foundation, Jean said the following: "Looking back over . . . the years, we found that we were most successful when we were fearless—when we have explored and experimented—and the least successful when fear or caution somehow became a dominant driver of decision-making."[10] This rings true for me as well when I look back at my life.

The Case Foundation has identified five essential elements of fearless risk-taking. These are certainly worthy of consideration. If you want to be a fearless risk-taker:

1. Make big bets and make history.
2. Be bold and take risks.
3. Make failure matter.
4. Reach beyond your bubble.
5. Let urgency conquer fear.

So is risk-taking a good thing or a bad thing? Well, yes. Not all risk is good, and not all risk is bad. This is where judgment comes into play, along with our own risk tolerance.

Although this will look different for each of us, I am convinced that we grow and benefit from taking decisive actions that move us beyond the familiar to the frontiers awaiting. A fear-based life is not worth living. The discomfort that comes from venturing into unknown waters brings with it, eventually, after we have gained confidence from the experience, a deep sense of well-being. Only by stretching ourselves can we begin to understand that we are more capable and that life is less perilous than we might imagine.

Blind and deaf, the amazing and courageous Helen Keller once mused, "Life is either a daring adventure or nothing." In his poem "George Gray," from *Spoon River Anthology*, Edgar Lee Masters captures our ambivalence regarding the risk in venturing out:

I have studied many times
The marble which was chiseled for me—
A boat with a furled sail at rest in a harbor.
In truth it pictures not my destination
But my life.
For love was offered me and I shrank from its
     disillusionment;
Sorrow knocked at my door, but I was afraid;
Ambition called to me, but I dreaded the chances,
Yet all the while I hungered for meaning in my life.
And now I know that we must lift the sail
And catch the winds of destiny
Wherever they drive the boat.
To put meaning in one's life may end in madness,
But life without meaning is the torture
Of restlessness and vague desire—
It is a boat longing for the sea and yet afraid.

Taking small risks is one way to move beyond our fears, to enlarge our world and to secure a life rich with meaning and true purpose. Don't overthink it. Remember when you first jumped off a diving board. It was both terrifying and confidence-boosting. Let's do it again!

TAKE ACTION:
Determining the Place of Risk in Your Life

Twenty years from now you will be more disappointed by the things you didn't do than by the ones you did. So throw off the bowlines, sail away from the safe harbor, catch the trade winds in your sails. Explore. Dream. Discover.

—H. JACKSON BROWN JR.

In your journal reflect on these questions and exercises:

• *Do you consider risk-taking positive or negative? Why?*

• *Which risk-taker do you admire? Why?*

• *On a scale of 1 to 5, where 1 indicates being totally risk-adverse and 5 means embracing risk fully, where are you? Where would you like to be?*

• *How did your family raise you to think about risk? How does it influence you today?*

- *What are some particular fears that your family instilled in you?*

- *What specific risk did you take as a child? How did it feel?*

- *What small shift would make a difference in the quality of your life? What holds you back from making it?*

- *Write down three things that would be out of your comfort zone yet would benefit your life. Consider doing one, and then reflect on how it felt.*

- *Over the course of the next seven days, take three small risks and reflect on these experiences.*

- *Describe both a good risk and a bad risk you took. What were the ramifications of each?*

- *Do you know someone who is reckless? Have you ever been reckless? How have these experiences influenced you?*

- *What holds you back from taking an action that you know you should take?*

— 8 —

Live an Integrated Life

I feel blessed. So many men and women search
and search but never find their passion, their
calling, the sense of mission that would ignite their
hearts and fill their lives with meaning and joy.
—Robert Mondavi,
celebrated Napa Valley winemaker

The crucial issue is not whether a student will be a
"science and technology person" or a "humanities and
social sciences person".... The critical issue is that
a person needs both types of skills and knowledge
to innovate and lead in a rapidly changing world.
—Mary Sue Coleman and John L. Hennessy,
presidents, respectively, University of Michigan
and Stanford University

Many of us had parents who saw their jobs as a means
to an end. Most children of the Great Depression never
had the luxury of considering that a job could be more than

a paycheck. The modern notion of following your passion was unheard of for most in previous generations. Back then, people believed that jobs served a specific purpose: to provide food, shelter, and clothing for their families. They never considered whether it made them come alive or whether they were pursuing a fully integrated life.

This resolute devotion to sheer labor was simply, and perhaps realistically, fear-driven. I need this job, period. There is certainly nothing wrong with viewing one's job as a means to support those entrusted to our care. Yet it can be damaging when the two worlds, life and work, become decoupled. I believe a big part of us dies if we fail to see any larger purpose in our labors. More worrisome still is when we compartmentalize and separate our values from our work.

So I am suggesting we aim to live a fully connected and integrated life. Yes, this is aspirational, since it is not possible for us to see every detail of living and working as part of one whole cloth. But it is a goal worth pursuing.

Each aspect of our lives evokes and expresses meaning and purpose. Everything reinforces everything else. No part of our life is truly separate from the other parts; all the parts matter and make up who we are. Yes, it is good to have healthy boundaries around areas of our lives in order to protect each part, but that does not mean that we have different identities in each of these settings. We should strive to be fully integrated beings. We should strive to develop a mindset that allows us to be whole. Our mission statement should encompass our full life, including work, leisure, family, service.

Cautionary tales abound in which individuals decoupled their highest values from their day-to-day labors. An extreme example might be the devout Lutheran Nazi prison guards who did not consider their "job," keeping Jews in subjugation, to be in conflict with their professed religious beliefs. When people consciously or subconsciously refuse to acknowledge such radical inconsistency, horrible things can occur. Such dualistic thinking has led to despicable behavior, acts of utter cruelty, and even mass genocide performed by "good" ordinary people.

It is fascinating to consider our times from the perspective of connectivity. Increasingly, we embrace a globally connected world, and yet tribalism or tight private communities of interest are on the rise. The head of the International Monetary Fund, Christine Lagarde, observes a "breakneck pattern of integration and interconnectedness that defines our time."[1] That is certainly a valid view, but the opposite can also be said to be true as well. The author Gillian Tett, in her book *The Silo Effect*, describes the phenomenon in this way:

> But while the world is increasingly interlinked as a system, our lives remain fragmented. Many large organizations are divided, and then subdivided into numerous different departments, which often fail to talk to each other—let alone collaborate. People often live in separate mental and social "ghettos," talking and coexisting only with people like us. In many countries, politics is polarized. Professions seem increasingly specialized, partly because technology keeps

becoming more complex and sophisticated and, is only understood by a tiny pool of experts.

There are many ways to describe this sense of fragmentation: people have used words like "ghettos," "buckets," "tribes," "boxes," "stovepipes." But the metaphor I find useful is "silo."[2]

So which is right? I believe both positions are equally valid and provable.

Young professionals today have options few of their parents could have imagined. People today think deeply about the meaning of work. In fact, research reports that millennials would choose a workplace that fostered purpose and meaning over a larger paycheck.[3] This is a significant shift in attitude. In my view, this is a long overdue corrective. As with any large reset, though, new problems arise. Today, many young people believe work is all about passion and doing what you love—nothing else—which can lead to distorted views of the value and nature of work. Drudgery is in fact part of certain tasks, but work can still have meaning if we approach it rightly.

Miya Tokumitsu, in an article for *Jacobin* magazine, challenges the contemporary obsession with doing what you love, arguing that it degrades work that is not driven by one's purpose. Such thinking can be narrow and elitist.[4] In *The Stone*, a forum for philosophers managed by the *New York Times*, Gordon Marino goes further, adding that the work-as-passion model "ignores the idea that work itself possesses an inherent value and, most importantly, severs the traditional connection between work, talent, and duty."[5]

The value of work is not limited to feeding the passion of the working person. If we take a holistic approach, there's more to it. All work can be meaningful, even when it is hard and challenging, with elements of drudgery and routine. The challenge is daring to consider that work, however difficult, can be purposeful.

When talking about work and life, I prefer the term *integrated* over *balanced*. I frankly don't believe accomplished people can ever live a balanced life. That said, there are "seasons" when your level of intensity in a job is modulated to suit the moment. For instance, when I served on the White House staff, the work was enriching but rigorous, with long hours. It was a season that had an expiration date stamped on it, and that made the intensity tolerable.

It's essential to have a philosophy that enables us to thrive in good times and bad, whether a job is "meaningful" or simply to put bread on the table. We should aim to be fully human and integrated, yet know that sometimes we simply show up and work our tail off. Work is often challenging, but that's not the point. We work to contribute and to be paid for that contribution. I love teaching at Georgetown University, bringing lessons from the real world as well as history and philosophy to enrich business students preparing to become tomorrow's leaders. It is energizing. But it is also very hard work at times, and that's just fine.

To live a fully integrated life, we need to keep in mind why we work. In the daily grind of work it is sometimes easy to lose sight of this. Sometimes what we need, in order to bring meaning to our vocations, is a holistic or bigger vision for what we do.

A story is told of a medieval pilgrim who asked two stone-masons about their work on Chartres Cathedral in France. When the first mason was asked what he was doing, he simply shrugged and said, "Building stone walls day after day. Pure drudgery." His sentiment mirrors a 2013 Gallup poll finding that, worldwide, only 13 percent of employees are engaged at work.[6] Some things don't change.

The second mason had a different answer: "What am I doing? I am creating a monument to the glory of God." Two masons were performing identical work, yet only one possessed an elevated vision of his labors, a view that animated him and gave purpose to his hard labor.

When a youthful President Kennedy arrived at Cape Canaveral for the first space launch, he asked a NASA employee about his job. "I am putting a man on the moon" was the man's proud reply. Only later did the president learn that the man was a janitor, a janitor with an inspired vision of his contribution to the larger effort.

Life is best lived when we experience it seamlessly and holistically, with body, mind, and spirit conspiring together for the good of the whole person. Pablo Picasso said, "It's not what an artist does that counts, but what he is." For him, what he did was who he was and vice versa. Would anything be better than such a seamless approach to work and living? Yet we live in a world that does its best to categorize, divide, and dispirit. We're often pushed to steer away from meaning in the workplace, to compartmentalize work and life to our detriment. The unfortunate result is that we view work as only a means to an end, rather than as an opportunity to express our giftedness in a work environment.

The intellectual and practical underpinnings of compartmentalization date way back in history. Certainly, the industrial revolution took mechanization and compartmentalization to new heights, viewing people as a means to an end, mere commodities. But this way of thinking predates even the nineteenth century. For centuries rulers used slave labor to build monuments and whole civilizations.

Still, some ancient cultures made the integration of different parts of our lives an ideal to aim for. Greek philosophy drew a distinction between the body and the spirit, but, as a practical matter, saw integrating these elements as important. For example, the Greeks saw exercise as essential for a life well lived. They would often spend a day at the *gymnasium*, or "gym," exercising while doing business, teaching, or trading.

Theologically, the Hebrews saw everything as sacred and good, including the body. In the book of Genesis, after each of the six successive days of creation, the Bible notes: "God saw that it was good."[7] Christians took this idea further, celebrating the Incarnation, in which God took on a human expression in Jesus, thereby elevating all of humanity as good and valuable. So rather than denigrating the body as evil and "sinful," as later theology maintained, the body and sexuality were originally seen as good, designed for our enjoyment and delight. Everything fits harmoniously in this way of thinking.

Sadly, the model of compartmentalization is deeply entrenched in many quarters, including some religious circles. Not viewing all of life as one delicious adventure, but rather assigning negative meaning to particular parts of it, leads to unfortunate outcomes. We make our lists—sex is bad, hard work is good. You get the drift. But it becomes tiresome and tedious. Wouldn't it be better to embrace all of life as wondrously interconnected, truly valuable, and good?

In his book *Working*, Studs Terkel compiled interviews with over one hundred people about their jobs. One of those interviews stood out for me. It was disturbing, and enlightening, and is relevant to our discussion here. Nora Watson, a young teacher, had come to her job with great enthusiasm. She was eager to shape young hearts and minds as a teacher. Unfortunately, she quickly found herself surrounded by fellow teachers who had divorced themselves from any belief that their work held much meaning for them. In fact, Watson felt penalized and ostracized for seeking to be an engaged teacher.

Sadly, she eventually determined that only one course was available to her. She joined her colleagues in living a pointless life, teaching lifeless lessons to lifeless students in a lifeless manner. At that point, she began to advance in her career. In her interview, she lamented, "I feel like I'm being pimped for and it's not my style. The level of bitterness in this department is stunning." She had hoped for more and then realized that her desire to bring all that she could to her work was not valued. With a few final words, she gave voice to a longing many of us can sympathize with: "There's nothing I would enjoy more than a job that was so meaning-ful to me that I brought it home."[8]

Inspired Work: Off the Walls and into the Halls

Intuitively, we humans want our lives and livelihoods to be in sync and integrated. There is far too little reflection, though, about what this means and how to go about it. How might we reward employees for being engaged? How do we best inte-grate work and life so that work is enriching even when it is hard or monotonous?

Although we might not be pausing enough to contem-plate such questions, it seems that cutting-edge businesses with true missions of purpose are catching on. New mod-els in finance, business, and technology are emerging, pro-ducing integrated business models that value people over profits. The cover story of the *Harvard Business Review* for

July–August 2018 is entitled "When Work Has Meaning." Authors Robert E. Quinn and Anjan V. Thakor state, "A higher purpose is not about economic exchanges. It reflects something more aspirational. It explains how the people involved with an organization are making a difference, gives them a sense of meaning, and draws their support."[9]

Bringing purpose to our labors can take various forms. Google gives its employees regular days off to focus on their own projects and even offers space for creative expression. The benefit is twofold: the individual feels inspired and autonomous, and the company becomes a place where bright, new ideas are born and integrated into its vital ecosystem.

Younger adult workers in particular want to be part of these reimagined work cultures, where life and work are seamlessly made to be a part of the entire work experience. Research shows that 71 percent of millennials want CEOs of large companies to use their positions for activism, compared to 46 percent of baby boomers. Millennials believe that corporate leaders have a responsibility to honestly speak to the important issues of the day. CEOs and other leaders have a platform and must use it.[10]

Starbucks founder Howard Schultz epitomizes this kind of leader. He says, "We are living in a world right now where every day, almost, some episodic event is affecting the way we live, the way we think, levels of anxiety, lack of trust, lack of confidence, polarization, dysfunction. How could we ignore what is going on? We have 350,000 people working for Starbucks—they expect Starbucks as a company to have a point of view about what we stand for, what our core purpose is, and what our reason for being is."[11]

Consciously or not, most long to be a part of a purpose-driven company. The celebrated winemaker Robert Mondavi intuitively understood this notion decades ago. He said, "Find a job you love, and you'll never have to work a day in your life."

Yes, we need work to support ourselves, but we also want companies to be authentic forces for good in a broader sense. We now aspire to be a part of a seamless work–life experience. Who does not desire a life trajectory in which we can bring our heart and talent in support of an enterprise that stands for a greater good beyond profit?

Author Erica Keswin, in *Bring Your Human to Work*, observes that millennials want to take aspirational mission statements "off the walls and into the halls"—they want to make it real.[12] This generation wants their work lives to have real meaning and thus looks to join companies with purpose where they can be part of something larger than themselves.

Nathaniel Koloc, cofounder of ReWork, writes that management consultants and Fortune 500 companies are saying the same thing about this generation of professionals: "They are not picking their next job based on the size of the paycheck. They are instead looking for a worthwhile mission and promising team to join."[13]

The real challenge for those unique purposeful CEOs and management teams has been to find practical ways to embed such high-minded thinking into the cultures of their firms.

KPMG, a Big Four accounting firm, found a way. Historically, the firm culture embraced "safe" (conservative) decision-making. But a shift occurred when the leadership realized that KPMG had made significant and notable historical contributions that ended up shaping world events. Based on these findings, the firm concluded that its purpose was to "Inspire Confidence. Empower Change." Now the challenge is driving such thinking into the very fabric of KPMG, lest it become a mere marketing gimmick.[14]

A program called the 10,000 Stories Challenge became the avenue to insinuate purpose-driven thinking and behavior throughout the firm. All employees were provided access to a user-friendly design tool to create posters answering the question: "What do you do at KPMG?" The intent was to capture employee passion and connect that to the overall vision of the firm.

Posters with headlines like "I Combat Terrorism" followed by a note of explanation and an employee picture were quickly produced by employees. Each poster had the firm's tagline: "Inspire Confidence. Empower Change." Surveys revealed that twenty-seven thousand employees had connected their personal purpose with that of the firm. This went beyond sentimentality, creating an environment where employees felt they were part of something bigger that mattered. This, in turn, elevated KPMG to the number-one position in the Big Four accounting firms, with turnover much reduced and recruitment way up. So it can be done.

A Lifestyle of Integration

Leonardo da Vinci is widely recognized as the greatest talent of his age, or of any age for that matter. Author Walter Isaacson recently mused about what made da Vinci so compelling and special.[15] Certainly, Isaacson observed, part of the answer has to do with da Vinci's view that all of life was connected in some fashion. He was a student of math, engineering, theater, optics, geology, and architecture as well as numerous other disciplines. All of this varied knowledge and insight came together to shape one of the greatest artists and creative souls in history.

His unique way of connecting knowledge was and is unprecedented. During the time when he was painting his celebrated work *Mona Lisa*, da Vinci spent evenings at the morgue of Santa Maria Nuova hospital in Florence, Italy. Da Vinci was peeling the flesh off cadavers' faces to better appreciate muscles and nerves. "He became fascinated about how a smile begins to form," noted Isaacson. No doubt these insights helped da Vinci capture the elusive smile depicted in the *Mona Lisa*. He melded science and art in original ways.

Despite his enormous body of work, he was criticized by some for failing to focus only on his art. They felt he was distracted by his voracious appetite for learning and detail. But da Vinci understood what modern researchers are only now coming to recognize: great human achievement often occurs when we elevate our thinking from the immediate task at hand, whether through leisure activities or a broader array of seemingly unrelated distractions.

For example, Galileo laid the groundwork for the pendulum clock, and modern timekeeping, many years after watching an altar lamp swinging in a cathedral. Ironically, critics thought Einstein was distracted from important scientific pursuits when he played the violin. Great minds embrace a lifestyle of integration, understanding that insights and discoveries frequently arise by associations in different parts of the brain, often when we appear "distracted" and unfocused.

These days, people are beginning to realize that an integrated approach can lead to exciting breakthroughs. In art, design, neurology, theoretical physics, music, and particularly health care, models of integration are becoming more prevalent. Everything is connected in some fashion. For instance, it shouldn't surprise us that physical exercise is just as valuable for our emotional well-being as for our physical bodies. Exercise helps control elevated blood pressure, but it's also the best defense against memory deterioration and depression along with many other maladies that have for too long been viewed in isolation. Consider this: even a simple exercise routine like daily walking can make you 81 percent more creative.[16]

Steve Jobs, Mark Zuckerberg, Beethoven, Goethe, and Charles Darwin all saw benefits in extended walks, intuitively knowing that movement is essential to both well-being and productivity. Darwin sometimes walked an astounding thirty miles in a day! More and more we need to bring this same understanding to the world of business. Everything is essentially connected: body, mind, and spirit.

An existential crisis can prompt introspection leading to a more complete and integrated life experience. Sometimes familiar life strategies fail us, forcing us to look elsewhere for guidance and inspiration. Winston Churchill faced such a moment when he was dismissed from his lofty position as Lord of the Admiralty over the Dardanelles failure during World War I; he became depressed and felt lost. It was then that he found a path of restoration and expression through painting.

I discovered this about Churchill while browsing the shelves in a small bookstore in Virginia decades ago. I had picked up a small book by the great man entitled *Painting as a Pastime*. The book was extracted from an essay Churchill wrote in the 1920s. In it, he candidly shares: "I had great anxiety and no means of relieving it. . . . I had long hours of utterly unwonted leisure in which to contemplate the frightful unfolding of the War. At a moment when every fibre of my being was inflamed to action, I was forced to remain a spectator of the tragedy, placed cruelly in a front seat."[17] Churchill had recently faced not only a very public and humiliating dismissal but had long battled a form of depression he called the "black dog."

Spiraling farther down each day, Churchill made an important and timely discovery that brought renewed hope. He recounts: "And then it was that the Muse of Painting came to my rescue." In one sense, painting was a "reset" for Churchill.

He could become fully absorbed in his new delight, turning his active mind off and letting go of the self-doubts, the bitterness, and the regrets. He notes, "Painting is complete as a distraction. I know of nothing which, without exhausting the body, more entirely absorbs the mind."[18]

I believe that painting saved Churchill. It provided him with a new way to understand life and his place in it. Painting fueled a transformation. He became creative and forceful, and in this renewed state he had his second act in public service, defeating the Nazis during World War II and saving Western civilization. Who would have thought that landscape portraiture would be the salvation of one of the greatest leaders in modern times?

The ways to integration and wholeness are many and varied. But wholeness is an aspirational goal that we strive to reach, much like Odysseus's long journey to Ithaca in *The Odyssey*. Ithaca represents the ultimate destination we yearn to reach our entire lives. In a previous chapter, my focus was upon the power and importance of forgiveness as central to a life of thriving. But did you know that forgiveness is also important to actually moving forward, letting go of the past, and restoring your wholeness?

One extraordinary thing arising from South Africa's dark days of apartheid was the establishment of the Truth and Reconciliation Commission, chaired by Nobel laureate Bishop Desmond Tutu. The commission's operating principle was "The truth sets you free." If individuals who did unspeakable things during that racist era would honestly confess their wrongdoing, they would be forgiven and not held criminally liable for past conduct. This was a significant departure from anything previously done in such circumstances. And it worked. Hundreds confessed to horrible crimes and were then forgiven. The culture was able to make peace with a history of horror without descending into vengeful blood-letting. Through confession and forgiveness they could find wholeness.

This commission pioneered a new way for nations to move beyond horrific experiences of civil conflict, oppression, and even genocide. Tutu believes that all need forgiveness in order to experience grace and true liberation. He says, "In our own ways, we are all broken. Out of that brokenness, we hurt others. Forgiveness is the journey we take toward healing the broken parts. It is how we become whole again."[19] Research finds that forgiving transforms us mentally, emotionally, spiritually, and even physically. To be whole, we all need to forgive and be forgiven. It is another way to restore what has been taken from us.

You don't need a crisis to embrace an integrated lifestyle. Are their creative outlets that inspire you? Are you taking the time to explore those possibilities? Is there time in your life to walk, to think, to write, to meditate, to pursue creative expressions? Whom do you need to forgive? Do you bring imagination and care for those different from yourself into the workplace?

Get Out of Your Comfort Zone

By now, you've no doubt seen that all my questions relate to the others. Integrated living necessitates that we embrace the entire picture. Our previous discussion of risk certainly relates to living such an integrated life. You can't live an integrated life without some risk-taking. Moving into unknown territory isn't easy, but it is the doorway to accessing a richer life experience. Imagine Churchill's fear as he lifted his paintbrush the first time. Once you extend your boundaries and learn that risk is your friend, deep satisfaction and a new confidence await.

In 2016, I went with a small group to dine at a restaurant in London called Dans Le Noir, French for "in the dark." The restaurant is run by blind people, and the entire meal is experienced in complete and utter darkness. Your blind waiter guides you throughout the meal. As in the silent retreat, this can be quite scary and disorienting, particularly for controlling, high-functioning individuals.

Denying yourself a familiar window to reality is very, very challenging. Yet by shutting off your sense of sight, other senses become more acute and attuned to all that's around you. Hearing and touch are alert in new ways. Few are prepared for this type of letting go, denying such an important sense as sight. It is a risk. But by venturing out, fresh personal insights come into sharp focus. The evening at Dans Le Noir was wonderfully unsettling and certainly took each of us to a new place in our quest for integration, seeing with "new" eyes.

It is important to pursue an integrated life, but it won't be a smooth ride. In the toughest times, it certainly helps to have some faith or philosophy that guides and anchors you. While a graduate student, I was jogging past the Bodleian Library in Oxford, England. I was in a foul mood since my research thesis had hit a rough patch. I turned a corner and there before me stood fellow student Margaret Falatico. I slowed down to say hello but was in no frame of mind for a chat.

Margaret, clearly seeking to engage in something deep, said, "Doug, you seem to have a peace and joy in your life. Is that because you jog?"

I blurted out a feeble yes and then continued on my way. Then my conscience intervened. I recalled the story of Peter, who denied Jesus three times. Yikes!

I pivoted and jogged back in her direction. Now, standing squarely in front of her, I muttered quietly, "Margaret, yes, jogging helps in the peace and joy department, yet I also found an anchor—not in dogma, but in a living faith. I am in a terrible mood since my thesis is struggling, but let's discuss if and when I resurface."

I guess on a certain level, the jogging in fact did contribute to my peace of mind, but there was much more to it. Faith has played a central role in my objective to live an integrated life. It has been a compass in the most difficult of moments.

Certainly, there are always forces working against the goal of an integrated life. We spend our days not sure why we are chasing certain things. Is it because of our culture and peers that we pursue various aims or for other complex reasons? We strive for one achievement after the other, without necessarily considering the rationale for our mindless questing for more.

Doing for just the sake of doing can kill the spirit inside. The most widely read article ever published in the *New Republic* was an essay by William Deresiewicz from his book entitled *Excellent Sheep: The Miseducation of the American Elite and the Way to a Meaningful Life*. The article focused on how, a century ago, universities shaped the character of young leaders by focusing on the elements of a purposeful life. Today, the ground has shifted, and we live in a résumé-crazed culture.[20]

David Brooks wrote an article for the *New York Times* elaborating on Deresiewicz's piece. Brooks observed of today's youth, "The system pressures them to be excellent, but excellent sheep." Brooks argues that universities have been transformed by the commercial ethos. They are breeding grounds for getting ahead. Brooks notes, "Students are too busy jumping through the next hurdle in the résumé race to figure out what they really want. . . . They have a terror of closing off options. They have been inculcated with a lust for prestige and a fear of doing things that may put their status at risk."[21]

This may seem overly harsh, but it is worrisome to think that future leaders are being shaped in such a mechanistic way. I hope that Deresiewicz and Brooks only partially understand the story. We live in a time with many contradictions.

My MBA students long for ways to live engaged integrated lives, with impact and significance beyond résumé building. More and more of my students realize the utter bankruptcy in accumulating accolades devoid of any meaning. Mahatma Gandhi articulated such a view that the "means [one's profession] are ends for [a meaningful life]."

The Trinity Forum, based in the Washington area, offers programs and publications to help leaders engage life's important questions in the context of faith. Some years ago, it brought to my attention an excerpt from an essay by Arthur Applbaum, of Harvard Law School, called "Professional Detachment: The Executioner of Paris." Applbaum presents a fictitious exchange between a journalist and an executioner during the Reign of Terror in France (1793–94).[22] The journalist finds the executioner despicable for understandable reasons—for openers, he lops off heads for a living. The journalist argues that since the executioner and his family have beheaded enemies of the state for four generations, they are the utter scum of the earth.

Yet the executioner's retort is compelling. He explains that violence needs to be controlled by the state. He defends his professionalism, noting that he and his family use clean baskets and sharp blades on every occasion. He further holds that the family remained apolitical, serving whichever political faction led the French government at any given moment.

It is a fascinating and disturbing conversation, in which the executioner makes a powerful case for viewing life and his profession holistically. So where do you draw the line? Should investment bankers represent tobacco companies or those who spoil the environment? I am not certain where I ultimately come out on this argument with regard to beheadings with a purpose. I do know we need to wrestle deeply with matters like this if we are to create new models that make workers and employees feel that they are part of something truly redemptive and not just working for a paycheck. Research supports the idea that meaning trumps money as a motivator in the workplace. Work is truly valuable, period, not just for the pay.

I love a section about one's vocation from a poem by W. H. Auden. He captures our innate longing that our life's work be one of true purpose and meaning. You know the truth of these lines when you read them:

You need not see what someone is doing
to know if it is his vocation,
you have only to watch his eyes:
a cook mixing a sauce, a surgeon
making a primary incision,
a clerk completing a bill of lading,
wear the same rapt expression,

forgetting themselves in a function.
How beautiful it is,
That eye-on-the-object look.[23]

People generally agree that a sense of purpose and meaning is good for the psyche. But did you know that having a purpose makes a real difference in our life expectancy, according to a study published in *The Lancet*?[24] This finding is just one more indication that life is an integrated whole in which everything affects everything else, reinforcing the urgency to find true purpose.

Leaders today need to understand how interconnected everything is. In spite of the new emphasis upon STEM education (an interdisciplinary approach that includes science, technology, engineering, and math), we should never marginalize the humanities with their historical perspectives and moral lessons drawn from the best and worst of our past. Wharton professor Stew Friedman tells us how leaders should think about their roles today: "Now more than ever leadership is not just about work, it's about life. Success in the new world of business requires us to see leadership and life as pieces of the same puzzle." He advocates "integrating work, home, community, and self—and improving performance in all these parts—by the powerful combination of increased authenticity (being real), integrity (being whole), and creativity (being innovative)."[25]

Does everything fit in your worldview?

TAKE ACTION:
Living an Integrated Life

Surveys confirm that meaning is the top thing
millennials say they want from a job. . . . What they
fail . . . to realize is that work can be meaningful
even if you don't think of it as a calling.

—EMILY ESFAHANI SMITH,
AUTHOR OF *THE POWER OF MEANING*

In your journal reflect on these questions and exercises:

• *Do you compartmentalize your life between the professional and the personal? How do you do that? List three small shifts you might make to reintegrate.*

• *Consider the purpose of your work, and write a short statement expressing it.*

• *Who do you know who is a good model of a person integrating life and work?*

• *Can business be a "high" calling?*

• *Do you think we overly emphasize finding a passion for young people? Does this set them up for failure and false expectations, or do you think it important for the good life?*

- *Is there a "perfect" job that you think would make you come alive?*

- *Is your life integrated? How so? What's lacking? How would friends answer this question about you?*

- *Is it too idealistic to think that a business can have a purpose beyond profits?*

Leave a Legacy

Here I am in the twilight years of my life,
still wondering what it's all about. . . . I can tell
you this, fame and fortune is for the birds.
—LEE IACOCCA, LEGENDARY AUTOMOTIVE CEO

Should you live for your résumé . . . or your eulogy?
—DAVID BROOKS, JOURNALIST

All of us will leave a legacy of some sort. Consider Rosie Ruiz, who recently died at age sixty-six. Her name will forever be associated with the 1980 Boston Marathon. Ms. Ruiz had her victory vacated after officials learned that she had snuck into the race only a mile before the finish. A victory would have given her the third fastest time ever by a woman. She sought one legacy and left quite another.

All of us, ordinary though we are, have the chance to make a difference and leave a legacy with our lives. In the gardens of Corpus Christi College at Oxford, there is a small plaque on a bench in memory of Russell Crockford (1957–81). It merely states this about young Crockford: "He did all that he could." I have puzzled over the meaning of this short epitaph on a couple of occasions and have concluded that it is indeed an inspirational charge to the rest of us. Though Crockford lived briefly, he lived to his potential, and that was enough.

Perhaps this epitaph holds the key for the rest of us. We should do all that we can, with all of the passion we can muster, and let others determine the worthiness of our contribution. We should stop fretting about the various audiences that we perceive have opinions about our lives; they likely don't care anyway. This fixation on seeking the approval of others is literally killing young people. The Instagram obsession to "shape" a narrative brings little satisfaction, since all know this is manufactured for public consumption, including the photoshopped pictures of ourselves.

We as leaders should model a different way, where we draw our sense of well-being and accomplishment from within. It takes courage to live this way. The added benefit of living for an "audience of one" is releasing the artificial, self-generated pressure and living authentically with purpose, not worrying about the results.

Most of us tend to avoid any serious consideration of our legacy, partially because it inevitably leads to questions of mortality and death. David Barnard, professor of ethics at Oregon Health and Science University, has written extensively on the end of life. His findings reveal that "a major part of American society is very averse to thinking about dying."[1]

And yet, at least with some, it seems that the tide has begun to turn. Death Cafes have been springing up all across America. Now in well over a hundred cities, these cafes are not for grief support or end-of-life planning, but rather for talking about the unmentionable, death, in casual settings. Jon Underwood, founder of the Death Cafe movement, notes, "There's a growing recognition that the way we've outsourced death to the medical profession and to funeral directors hasn't done us any favors." He sees the Death Cafe as "a space where people can discuss death and find meaning and reflect on what's important."[2]

In earlier times, death was always looming and ever present. Life was shorter, and few had either the time or the luxury to contemplate higher-order matters like their legacy. It was hard to escape the harsh reality of death, as seen in the writings of Kierkegaard and Socrates, among others. Accepting the reality of our demise, though, is different from thinking about the meaning of it all. Sitting down and talking about death, reflecting on it, will inevitably lead us to explore all sorts of issues, including our legacy. How will we be remembered?

Ultimately, others will determine if and what we contributed to the greater good during our lifetime. Still, it's useful to take stock and consider what you might hope your legacy to be, as long as you don't become obsessive and try to manipulate the messaging. How would you like to be remembered?

Several years ago, I heard of an exercise that brings together the two topics under consideration, death and legacy. A small group gathers, in which the members share a personal eulogy they have written for themselves, a statement of what they hope would be read at their funeral. This assignment forces everyone in the group to determine what they truly value and how they want to be honored. It mirrors David Brooks's notion of eulogy virtues over résumé virtues.

A twist on this exercise occurred in May 1897. Imagine if you opened the newspaper only to discover notice of your untimely passing. An overeager reporter made a crucial error in an article in the *New York Journal* about the celebrated author Mark Twain. He penned that Twain was dead. The story landed on the front page, where it immediately came to Twain's notice while he was staying in a London hotel. Apparently, Twain read that he passed away quietly in his home. Of the story, Twain quipped, "The reports of my death are greatly exaggerated."

On another occasion, several years earlier, in 1888, a French daily reported that Alfred Nobel, the Swedish inventor, had died in Cannes. It announced: "Dr. Alfred Nobel, who became rich by finding ways to kill more people faster than ever before, died yesterday." It also proclaimed, "The merchant of death is dead." The Nobel family had accumulated a fortune by inventing dynamite. This invention transformed modern warfare, enabling killing on a truly epic scale. It was a damning obituary, but it was about the wrong Nobel. Alfred had not died. Rather, it was his brother, Ludvig, who had passed while in the south of France.

Still, a shaken Alfred found the obituary deeply troubling. He was distraught that this epitaph might become his final legacy. So he proceeded to set aside the bulk of his estate to establish the Nobel Prizes; one of them, the Nobel Peace Prize, has been awarded to the likes of Mother Teresa, Martin Luther King Jr., and Nelson Mandela.

As Alfred Nobel demonstrated, it's never too late to alter our trajectory, so that it reflects our true purposes. A major trauma or setback often triggers self-reflection. Seize those wake-up calls. They bring us back to the essentials. As former White House Chief of Staff Rahm Emanuel said during the financial meltdown several years back, "A crisis is a terrible thing to waste."

It is easy to think of legacy in rather grand terms, comparing ourselves to the Churchills or Mandelas of the world and, by comparison, feeling like a failure. A statement by author Jack London puts pressure on us to do something truly significant with our brief time on this earth. London announced to the world:

I would rather be ashes than dust! I would rather that my spark should burn out in a brilliant blaze than it should be stifled by dry-rot. I would rather be a superb meteor, every atom of me in magnificent glow, than a sleepy and permanent planet. The proper function of man is to live, not to exist. I shall not waste my days in trying to prolong them. I shall use my time.[3]

London's passionate call to action can feel a bit intimidating. The notion that one should be a "superb meteor," never wasting a moment—now that's a high bar. But there's surely a place for a legacy from each one of us. We won't all shine the same way, naturally.

Earlier I mentioned that, while on the White House staff, I had occasion to meet and spend time with Mother Teresa. To my question about what it was like to be Mother Teresa, she responded humbly, acknowledging her human vulnerabilities. This celebrated woman, small in stature with a radiant smile, who considered herself an "ordinary" human being, hoped that her time on earth made some difference. It certainly did. But the real hope she gives us is that all of us can make some difference.

When you think about legacy, use a holistic approach. Think about the things in your life that truly matter, the essence of what you value. The chair of the global public-relations firm WPP, Phil Lader, is a longtime friend. Phil has lived an amazing life of accomplishment, including serving as ambassador to the Court of St. James's in England.

He observes that leaders are accustomed to juggling many balls. Most of those balls are rubber and, if dropped, have little real consequence. But, Phil goes on to say, some balls are crystal and, if dropped, shatter with great effect. Those precious balls are family, health, and a few other truly valuable things. Pay attention to the precious crystal balls, lest one be dropped and you suffer real harm. How you handle those crystal balls can play a big role in the legacy you pass on.

Phil's metaphor calls to mind a concept that Stephen Covey outlined in his bestseller *The 7 Habits of Highly Effective People*. Covey urges us to keep the end in mind by putting into our "life jar" the large rocks first. These rocks are the central things that matter most.[4] Too often, we are preoccupied with the minutiae of life. We are busy being busy, and we lose sight of those foundational things. We fill our jars with smaller rocks in a way that leaves no room for the important larger stones. Reflecting on either the crystal balls or the larger rocks in our lives forces us to consider our lives in a different way, to step back and pinpoint what we care most about.

Those essential truths will be the ultimate statement, defining our lives and legacies. Are we investing our time and resources in what endures? Remember, during your lifetime, you should be the one prioritizing how to invest your time and resources, not some other audience. Release yourself from the unrelenting pressure to please. That obsession pushes us to live another's definition of success and thriving, not our own. No matter how gifted, wealthy, or beautiful you are, you'll never feel you have done enough if you accept another's narrative and fail to create your own. In an interview with film legend Cary Grant, the interviewer observed that every man wants to be Cary Grant. Grant quipped, "Yes, even I want to be Cary Grant."

As I mentioned in Chapter 6, we value letter-writing exercises at PathNorth. At the end of a gathering, we often have group members write a letter to themselves, which is later mailed to them. You can use a variation of this practice for yourself. After a period of introspection, when you have wrestled with some important questions, write a letter to yourself outlining your insights, conclusions, or thoughts for the future. Put it in an envelope, address it, and have someone mail it to you a month later, a year later, or whenever you decide. When the letter arrives, it'll bring you back to the right questions and remind you of an earlier moment of clarity.

Anytime you put pen to paper, it slows you down to nail what you truly care about, which is important in fashioning a legacy. This process will help you become more centered. It will also prompt a thought or two about legacy.

Robber baron Andrew Carnegie took time from his frantic business pursuits to write such a letter to himself in December 1868. It was a remarkable document for a young man of thirty-three to record. Two lines from this famous piece jump out at me. First, his view of money: "Man must have an idol and the amassing of wealth is one of the worst species of idolatry! No idol is more debasing than the worship of money!" The other interesting point was his goal to cap his earnings: "Make no effort to increase my fortune, but spend the surplus each year for benevolent purposes! Let us cast aside business forever, except for others."[5] Carnegie saw clearly what he wanted his legacy to look like, yet he failed in its execution. This is a reminder to anchor our lofty ambitions in some form of accountability, lest we too fail to live up to our noblest intentions.

Make It Count

Ten years ago, the CEO of Regal Boats in Florida sent me a curious gift, a glass vase filled with marbles. In a note, he said he had estimated my age, made a rough calculation of how many years I had remaining, and filled the jar accordingly. He then urged me to remove one marble each month. This would remind me of the brevity of life and to make it count. This calls to mind what the seventeenth-century poet John Donne did to keep perspective. Donne supposedly kept a human skull on his desk. It was a constant reminder: "Life is short; do something with it."

I have always been impressed by individuals who seem to know, often at an early age, a precise life objective or calling. I have already mentioned one of my heroes and inspirations, the eighteenth-century British reformer William Wilberforce. A truly remarkable individual, he successfully led the abolitionist movement that eventually banned slavery from the British Empire. One British historian described the abolition of slavery, led by Wilberforce, as "one of the turning points in the history of the world."

Wilberforce found his calling for this dangerous and daunting task in his early twenties, and he never wavered from that path. A journal entry of his on October 28, 1787, declares: "God Almighty has set before me two great objects, the suppression of the slave trade and the reformation of manners [i.e., morals]."[6] His mentor John Wesley, the founder of Methodism, warned him of the personal cost of assuming this difficult calling, saying, "Unless God has raised you up for this very thing, you will be worn out by the opposition of men and devils."[7]

Still, Wilberforce soldiered on, knowing this was the very mission for which he was born. His calling became his life's work and, eventually, his legacy. To add even more poignancy to this story, Wilberforce died three days after Parliament passed legislation to abolish the slave trade. It was an unprecedented decision, rooted in moral courage, to go against the economic interests of the entire British Empire.

As someone who has never had such a specific calling, I am always impressed and intrigued by others who have. When he was in the US Senate, former vice president Al Gore invited me to lunch in his office. While we talked, I learned about his own life calling to protect the environment. Whatever one might think of his politics or his views on global warming, his passion and knowledge about the environment are undeniable. I asked him when he knew this was his calling. It was in the fifth grade! How does that happen?

The answer to the question of what we should do with our lives isn't always readily apparent. I have had many young professionals come to my office to discuss how to go about finding their calling or life's work. Frankly, it is often the blind leading the blind, but I do have a few exercises that some have found helpful in solving this puzzle. Surprisingly, the answer is often hiding in plain sight, since our strengths and likes are frequently unconscious, yet surface repeatedly over our lifetimes. I ask these folks to consider two questions, as they look at their lives spanning from their earliest memories to the present: What did you love to do? What did others say you were good at? It's amazing how revealing these two simple questions can be.

In my kindergarten class, each day following recess, a tall girl named Judy Rich would line us up by height and then present us to the teacher. No one asked Judy to do this; it was in her DNA. I am sure that Judy, if indeed she found her calling, is an accountant or actuary, since precision metrics and organizing seemed to make her come alive.

Another exercise that I propose to young professionals in search of their calling is to break their lives into five-year periods: age one to five, five to ten, ten to fifteen, and so on. Think about those intervals. What did you love doing and knew you were naturally good at? What made you come alive in each of them? Was it working as part of a team or alone? Was it learning to write or speak in front of others? Did you like working with your hands? Were you a problem-solver whom others sought out? Did you relish leading or following? You get my point. How you are wired shows up early. I am convinced that if you answer those questions and apply that understanding of yourself throughout life, you have a much better shot at finding what you were intrinsically meant to do. And, by extension, this leads to fashioning an authentic legacy, one true to you and how you are wired.

One more way people can explore what their calling might be is a schematic consisting of two large circles side by side with some overlap in the middle. In one circle go their passions, the things that have always made them come alive—art, piano, writing, sports broadcasting, and so on. In the other circle are the more pragmatic necessities, the things they must do to make a living, the responsibilities they must handle.

If one is fortunate, there is the possibility, not probability, that those two circles might overlap and you actually get paid for doing what you love. It is not a foregone conclusion, but it certainly could occur if you maintain a clear, resolute vision in your heart and mind of what you truly want. Yet if you have no picture of where you would like to end up, you are unlikely to see those hopes materialize.

A caveat here, though. It may not be possible to find that overlap, that dream job, right off the bat. Initially, we will need to spend most of our time on the things in that pragmatic circle, the things we have to do to make a living. But we should not neglect the items in the passion circle, the things we care about deeply, the things that make us feel alive. Yes, we should be pragmatic and support ourselves, but continue to invest in those passions, even if with limited time.

I once heard a story of a woman who for decades was a backup to the lead singer at the Met in New York City. Finally, her moment arrived when the virtuoso took ill, and she had to fill in for the remainder of the season. Working as a waitress all those years, she had been waiting for her chance, but she was now one of the lucky ones who gets paid for doing what she loves.

Another approach is what I challenge my MBA students to do at the conclusion of each class. I ask them to write a three- to four-page essay (which counts for 50 percent of their grade) in which they have a conversation with their twenty-five-year-older selves, asking questions and getting advice, over a good bottle of Bordeaux. If you try this, what is the older you urging the younger you to value and pay attention to in the intervening decades? This will hopefully help you differentiate what truly matters from what seems utmost in the urgency of the moment. Legacy is constructed from such thinking.

As another exercise, take the time to write down a set of principles to guide your life. This might seem theoretical, but it can have real impact on your behavior and priorities. In essence, it serves as a road map for the years ahead.

I learned a valuable lesson about defining one's principles while serving in government. In 1987, I accepted a position with Goldman Sachs in New York. Prior to moving, I had worked with the former chair of Goldman Sachs, John

Whitehead, who was then Deputy Secretary of State. I had not informed John that I was interviewing with his former firm and had, in fact, accepted an offer. After such a close personal and working relationship with John, I dreaded the meeting I'd scheduled to tell him about my decision.

Entering Whitehead's cavernous Foggy Bottom office, I nervously blurted out my decision. After his initial surprise, John directed me to a small couch with a credenza close by. He opened the drawer and removed a sheet of paper entitled "Goldman Sachs Business Principles." He'd written those in 1954. These principles had shaped the culture and value system of the firm for decades.

Interestingly, they focused more on matters of character and good practice than on how to make money. I felt a bit awkward as John stood in front of me and carefully read each principle. After he finished, he said that the most important thing I could do while at the firm was to live these principles and remind people at the firm to do likewise. For John, monetary rewards were merely the fruit of doing business the right way. I will never forget his passion and belief in holding to those ideals. It made a true impact on me as a young professional. His legacy and view of culture powerfully shaped me and countless others.

The path to creating a lasting legacy is also the path to becoming more aligned with our authentic selves. It brings to mind a favorite poem, "Who Am I?," by activist and martyr Dietrich Bonhoeffer, who was executed by the Nazis in 1945.

In the poem Bonhoeffer gives voice to the inner conflict most of us experience in trying to live an authentic life with purpose. We know that we are not the same person we project to the world and that we are all frauds on some level:

> *Am I really what others tell me?*
> *Or am I only what I myself know of me? . . .*
> *Who am I? This or the other?*
> *Am I then, this today and the other tomorrow?*
> *Am I both at the same time? In public, a hypocrite*
> *and by myself, a contemptible, whining weakling?*[8]

Some years ago, someone had the bright idea to interview individuals in their late eighties, asking them to speak to the question: "If you had your life to live over, how would you live it?" Nadine Stair, age eighty-five, wrote a poem that is now widely circulated. A few of the things she notes:

> *I'd try to make more mistakes next time.*
> *I would relax.*
> *I know of very few things I would take seriously.*
> *I would be crazier.*
> *I would have more actual problems and fewer imaginary*
>   *ones.*

When you are in your eighties, how will you reflect upon your past practices? Perhaps this is a good moment to pause and consider what you would do differently today as you shape tomorrow's legacy.

We all seek to finish well, to leave an enduring legacy that inspires others to be better, particularly for the sake of our families. The importance of one's legacy came home to me in 1988 at a private luncheon at the home of former secretary-general of the UN and Austrian president Kurt Waldheim. Waldheim had been revered as one of the great leaders of the twentieth century, until it was discovered that during World War II, while a young man, he had some connection, like so many others, as a minor functionary with the Third Reich. The ensuing scandal was devastating. Waldheim quickly became an international pariah. He was no longer welcome in the United States.

Several friends of mine in the German Parliament continued to associate with him and arranged a meeting for Waldheim and me at his lovely country home outside Vienna. Near the end of our luncheon, Waldheim asked if we might share a private moment in his study. Curious, I accepted.

A very emotional Waldheim explained how he had been unfairly accused and tried in the court of public opinion. After a distinguished life of public service, he was indeed a broken man. Then he asked me a question. Would I arrange for a prominent American Jew to privately meet with him, to at least hear his side of the story? Since Waldheim knew of my connection with Goldman Sachs, he assumed that I would know such a person.

I promised to try. Upon returning to New York, I met with Bob Rubin, the Goldman Sachs chair, a fine man with a brilliant mind. Bob would eventually become the US Secretary of the Treasury. After I told Bob about Waldheim's emotional plea, he tentatively agreed to the proposed meeting. Not surprisingly, after Bob's family learned of the plan, they strongly objected. There was obvious concern that, in such a highly charged atmosphere, even a simple act of listening to one man's version of history could be misconstrued as tacit approval of unspeakable acts by the Nazis.

At least, I felt, I had kept faith with my promise to try. I had many thoughts and feelings about this experience, but above all I saw before me a man desperate not to let his critics define his legacy. For the sake of his family and for his own peace of mind, he wanted to have the final say.

In a sense, we'd all like to write our own history to set the record straight. But is that truly worth any effort? Like Carnegie, we might have lofty aspirations and goals, but we can always count on our humanness to eventually assert itself.

The story of the Apostle Paul is illustrative. Paul had been a relentless opponent of the movement surrounding Jesus of Nazareth and even participated in the murder of some of Jesus's followers. Eventually, though, Paul had an epiphany and became an ardent follower of Christ. Not surprisingly, many of the original believers didn't trust Paul's newfound faith. As is our human tendency, Paul wanted to set things right, to convince others of his genuineness and altered purpose. After all, he was a changed man. But nearing the end of his life, Paul no longer felt any need to correct the record. He merely concluded, "By the grace of God, I am what I am."[9] There was no need to fight old battles and convince others of his worthiness.

So too with us. The following poem by Thomas Merton gives voice to the many contradictions and longings embedded in our stories. But by the grace of God, we are what we are.

> *My Lord God,*
> *I have no idea where I am going.*
> *I do not see the road ahead of me.*
> *I cannot know for certain where it will end.*
> *Nor do I really know myself,*
> *and the fact that I think I am following your will*
> *does not mean that I am actually doing so.*
> *But I believe that the desire to please you*
> *does in fact please you.*
> *And I hope I have that desire in all that I am doing.*
> *I hope I will never do anything apart from that desire.*
> *And I know that if I do this you will lead me by the right*
> *   road,*
> *though I may know nothing about it.*
> *Therefore I will trust you always,*
> *though I may seem to be lost and in the shadow of death.*
> *I will not fear, for you are ever with me,*
> *and you will never leave me to face my perils alone.*[10]

TAKE ACTION:
Choosing and Working on Your Legacy

Don't ask what the world needs. Ask what makes you come alive, and go do it. Because what the world needs is people who have come alive.
—HOWARD THURMAN

In your journal reflect on these questions and exercises:

- *Whose legacy do you admire? How does their contribution inspire you?*

- *What was the legacy of your parents? Do you believe they felt they made a difference? In what way?*

- *In two paragraphs write the ideal eulogy for yourself, one that you would be proud to have read at your funeral. How does that eulogy serve as a measure of the life you are living now?*

- *Gather a few friends and have them write the ideal eulogy they would want read at their funerals. Read them aloud to each other and discuss.*

- *On a sheet of paper list your passions in one column and your modes of earning a living in another. Do the lists have any overlap? Are you keeping the passions alive even if you don't get paid for them? Commit at least ten minutes per week to express one passion.*

- *Make another list of your passions and then list your obligations. Is there a passion that you have been neglecting? Take two small steps this week to make this passion a priority.*

- *Do you feel pressure to do something "grand" or "significant" with your life? Are you placing pressure on your children to do the same?*

- *Is our legacy something we can shape, or is it for others to determine?*

Conclusion:
Navigating Our Way

Good businesspeople ask one question: What is the problem we are trying to solve? Applying that formulation to my book, I ask: What problem is my book attempting to address? I have suggested that an epidemic of loneliness and disconnection afflicts a majority of Americans, particularly those in leadership. Simply put, many are lost and uncertain where to turn for help. It seems that so many of the institutions and mediating structures that once offered support have far less credibility and appeal in our times. Today we are both disconnected and lost . . . searching.

So what does it mean to be lost? The term evokes all sorts of disturbing images from despondency to recklessness. Let's unpack this a bit.

Sitting in church one Sunday, I listened as the tall British vicar reminded us that next Sunday's sermon would be special, targeted to the "lost." He urged that we bring our "lost" friends and neighbors to next week's service. I had two problems with the cleric's charge. First, what if some lost souls, by mistake, stumbled into today's service rather than into the one for their "kind" next Sunday? Would we bar them entry, telling them to return with next week's unwashed legion of lost souls?

But my second and more serious concern was with the definition of the word *lost*. In Luke 15, Jesus describes three instances of lostness: the lost coin, the lost sheep, and the lost son (also known as the prodigal son). The biblical use of the term *lost* does not carry pejorative baggage; it simply means "out of place." For instance, the coin was supposed to be in the purse, yet was out of place, lost. The one sheep was separated from the ninety-nine, again lost. And the prodigal son broke from the family, lost.

Returning to the vicar's challenge of who exactly is lost, I guess my answer would be "I am" and "Perhaps you are as well." Despite my attempts to live the right way, I fail miserably and regularly. I lose my way and am frequently out of place, lost. English author J. B. Phillips offers a helpful perspective on this matter of lostness: "The real danger . . . lies not in the more glaring and grosser temptations and sins, but in a slow deterioration of vision, a slow death to daring, courage, and the willingness to adventure."[1] That, my friends, is a description of lostness.

Since we all have this propensity to get lost, what are we to do? Perhaps the Greeks might lend a hand. In Greek mythology, the Minotaur was a creature, half man and half bull, that devoured humans for sustenance and resided in the depths of a dark cave at the center of a complicated labyrinth. The Athenian hero Theseus was determined to rescue the Athenian boys held by the Minotaur. His challenge was to enter this treacherous space, find and kill the beast, and lead the young men to freedom.

Although the beast was formidable, he was not the most difficult challenge awaiting. The labyrinth itself posed the greatest threat to the accomplishment of his dangerous mission. With its twists and turns in the darkness coupled with its seductive appeal to the senses, it was almost impossible for Theseus to navigate. It would be easy to become lost. Yet Ariadne, the king's daughter, who was in love with Theseus, offered a clever solution to keep her prince from becoming lost forever. She supplied him a ribbon that he could tie to the entrance of the labyrinth. He could hold the other end tightly, unspooling the ribbon as he ventured deeper, navigating the complex, dangerous maze. After killing the Minotaur, all Theseus had to do was retrace his steps, gripping the ribbon tightly, and follow the path to freedom. Brilliant!

Life is a dangerous labyrinth, ready to snare, misdirect, and seduce at every turn. All of its challenges are designed with one intention, that we lose heart, give up, and stay lost. Like Theseus, we need a tight grasp on a ribbon for direction when we can't see the way ahead. We've all been there. I hope that my book and the questions I have offered throughout might generate some insights, strategies, and real hope to help you find your way to a life of flourishing, a life not devoid of pain and failure but one full of meaning, authenticity, and connectedness. Thank you for going on the journey with me, a fellow "seeker" attempting to be a "wounded healer."

Carpe diem.

Never stop questioning.

—ALBERT EINSTEIN

Acknowledgments

Life is such a rich tapestry of relationships and experiences. I have benefited from each soul who has shown up at the right moment to encourage and challenge me along the way. I'm grateful to each one. You made me better.

My mentors and inspirations are some of the finest people I have ever known, they include: Chuck Reinhold, Judge Martin Bostetter, Heinz Christian Prechter and family, Doug Coe, Senator Charles Percy, Dr. Donald Drew, Mark Percy, John Whitehead (State Department), James A. Baker (White House), Bud McFarland (NSC White House), Gene Fife, Geoff Boisi, Bob Rubin (all Goldman Sachs), Senator Bill Brock, Ray Chambers, Bill Milliken, Ted Leonsis and Paul Almeida (Georgetown U.), Howard Peck, Mike Ullman, Jim Seneff, Dan Hord, and the HEB Foundation.

And close friends and family, what would I do without you? Bob and Nan Woody, Abraham and Salem Fiseha, Steve and Jean Case, my sister Sandra, Dan Webster, John and Susan Yates, Imam Magid, Ambassador Mary Ourisman, Dale Jones, Elizabeth Sims, Skip Ryan, Julia and Ryan, Caitlin and Hays, Kempe, Ann, Kay James, Secretary and Mrs. John Dalton, Craig and Connie Weatherup, Joe Gregory, General Kicklighter, Frank D'Souza, Bob Franklin (Morehouse), Bill Harrison, Mike and Holly Depatie, Carol Melton, Wayne Huizenga Jr., Mike Kane, Juan Edgar Picado, Tom Morgan, Ambassador Father Ron Anton, and our PathNorth team and members as well as my Windy Gap brothers and my New York friends in the Links/ Whitehead breakfast.

Lastly, certain gifted individuals showed me that ideas and imagination enrich life and work, bringing perspective to everything: Dan Case, Dr. John Walsh (Oxford), Dr. Os Guinness, Bill Mayer (Aspen Institute), Raj Shah (Rockefeller Foundation), Ambassador Akbar Ahmed, David Brooks, Tim Shriver, Mike Gerson, Judy Woodruff, Dr. Francis Collins (NIH), and my editor at HarperOne, Mickey Maudlin, and his able team, along with my agent, Jan Baumer.

Notes

Introduction

1. Login George and Crystal L. Park, "Meaning in Life as Comprehension, Purpose, and Mattering: Toward Integration and New Research Questions," *Review of General Psychology* 20, no. 3 (June 2016), https://www.researchgate.net/publication/304032002 _Meaning_in_Life_as_Comprehension_Purpose_and_Mattering _Toward_Integration_and_New_Research_Questions.

2. David Brooks, "Should You Live for Your Résumé . . . or Your Eulogy?," TED Talk, March 2014, https://www.ted.com/talks/david_brooks_should_ you_live_for_your_resume_or_your_eulogy?language-en.

3. Alison Wood Brooks and Leslie K. John, "The Surprising Power of Questions," *Harvard Business Review*, May–June 2018, https://hbr .org/2018/05/the-surprising-power-of-questions.

4. Rainer Maria Rilke, *Letters to a Young Poet*, ed. Ray Soulard Jr. (Portland, OR: Scriptor Press, 1973), p. 14.

Chapter 1: The Illusions of Success

1. Robert A. Burton, "A Life of Meaning (Reason Not Required)," *New York Times*, September 5, 2016, https://www.nytimes.com/2016/09/05 /opinion/a-life-of-meaning-reason-not-required.html.

2. Jaruwan Sakulku and James Alexander, "The Impostor Phenomenon," *International Journal of Behavioral Science* 6, no. 1 (September 2011): 73–92, https://www.sciencetheearth.com/uploads/2/4/6/5/24658156 /2011_sakulku_the_impostor_phenomenon.pdf.

3. Sally C. Curtin, Margaret Warner, and Holly Hedegaard, "Increase in Suicide in the United States, 1999–2014," *NCHS Data Brief*, no. 241, April 2016, https://www.cdc.gov/nchs/data/databriefs/db241.pdf.

4. Clayton M. Christensen, "How Will You Measure Your Life?," *Harvard Business Review*, July–August 2010, https://hbr.org/2010/07/how-will -you-measure-your-life.

5. Vivek Murthy, "Work and the Loneliness Epidemic," *Harvard Business Review*, September 2017, https://hbr.org/cover-story/2017/09/work -and-the-loneliness-epidemic.

6. Robert Steven Kaplan, *What You're Really Meant to Do: A Road Map for Reaching Your Unique Potential* (Boston: Harvard Business School Publishing, 2013).

7. Cathy Free, "This Town's Solution to Loneliness? The 'Chat Bench,'" *Washington Post*, July 17, 2019, https://www.washingtonpost .com/lifestyle/2019/07/17/this-towns-solution-loneliness-chat -bench.

8. Tom Fox, "A Conversation with the NIH Director: On Overseeing Medical Breakthroughs, Making Music, and Riding a Harley," *Washington Post*, November 20, 2017, https://www.washingtonpost .com/news/on-leadership/wp/2017/11/20/a-conversation-with-the -nih-director-on-overseeing-medical-breakthroughs-making-music -and-riding-a-harley.

Chapter 2: Know Your Story

1. Elle Luna, *The Crossroads of Should and Must: Find and Follow Your Passion* (New York: Workman, 2015).

2. Robert Steven Kaplan, *What You're Really Meant to Do: A Road Map for Reaching Your Unique Potential* (Boston: Harvard Business School Publishing, 2013).

3. Thomas K. Houston et al., "Culturally Appropriate Storytelling to Improve Blood Pressure: A Randomized Trial," *Annals of Internal Medicine* 154, no. 2 (January 18, 2011): 77–84, doi: 10.7326/0003-4819 -154-2-201101180-00004.

4. Pedro M. Gardete, "Social Effects in the In-Flight Marketplace: Characterization and Managerial Implications," *Journal of Marketing Research* 52, no. 3 (June 2015): 360–74, https://www.gsb.stanford.edu/faculty-research/publications/social-effects-flight-marketplace-characterization-managerial.

5. Irving L. Janis, *Groupthink: Psychological Studies of Policy Decisions and Fiascos*, 2nd ed. (Boston: Cengage Learning, 1982).

6. David Riesman, *The Lonely Crowd* (New Haven, CT: Yale University Press, 2001).

7. Adam Grant, *Originals: How Non-Conformists Move the World* (New York: Penguin, 2016).

8. Bronnie Ware, *The Top Five Regrets of the Dying: A Life Transformed by the Dearly Departing* (Carlsbad, CA: Hay House, 2012).

9. Richard Rohr, *Falling Upward: A Spirituality for the Two Halves of Life* (San Francisco: Jossey-Bass, 2011).

Chapter 3: Maintain Genuine Relationships

1. David Brooks, "Startling Adult Friendships," *New York Times*, September 18, 2014, https://www.nytimes.com/2014/09/19/opinion/david-brooks-there-are-social-and-political-benefits-to-having-friends.html.

2. Gen. 2:18 (New International Version).

3. Hilary Weaver, "Michelle Obama Has Some Stern Words for Men, Barack Included," *Vanity Fair*, November 1, 2017, https://www.vanityfair.com/style/2017/11/michelle-obama-has-some-stern-words-for-men.

4. Jessica Stillman, "Loneliness: An Under-Diagnosed Epidemic Among New CEOs," *Inc.*, January 20, 2012, https://www.inc.com/jessica-stillman/loneliness-an-under-diagnosed-epidemic-among-new-ceos.html.

5. James D. Jameson and James C. Bottomley, *Across the Bars: Letters Between Two Friends* (Del Mar, CA: Wolfhouse Press, 2018).

6. Chris Pomorski, "'I Really Feel Most Comfortable in Prison': A Hedge Fund Ex-Con Finds It's Hard Coming Home to Greenwich," *Vanity*

Fair, July 2, 2019, https://www.vanityfair.com/news/2019/07/hedge
-fund-manager-chip-skowron-on-life-after-prison.

7. Olivia Laing, *The Lonely City: Adventures in the Art of Being Alone* (New
    York: Picador, 2016).

8. George E. Vaillant, *Triumphs of Experience: The Men of the Harvard
    Grant Study* (Cambridge, MA: Belknap, 2012), p. 27.

9. Steve Franklin and Lynn Peters Adler, *Celebrate 100: Centenarian
    Secrets to Success in Business and Life* (Hoboken, NJ: Wiley, 2013).

10. John T. Cacioppo and William Patrick, *Loneliness: Human Nature and
    the Need for Social Connection* (New York: W. W. Norton, 2008).

11. Gail Sheehy, *Understanding Men's Passages: Discovering the New Map
    of Men's Lives* (New York: Random House, 1998).

12. Thomas Merton, *No Man Is an Island* (New York: Image Books, 1967).

13. Prov. 27:17 (New King James Version).

14. Daryl Davis, "I Wanted to Understand Why Racists Hated Me. So I
    Befriended Klansmen," *Washington Post*, September 29, 2017, https://www
    .washingtonpost.com/outlook/i-wanted-to-understand-why-racists
    -hated-me-so-i-befriended-klansmen/2017/09/29/c2f46cb8-a3af-11e7
    -b14f-f41773cd5a14_story.html.

15. Dinah Maria Mulock Craik, *A Life for a Life* (1859; Project Gutenberg,
    2015), vol. 2, http://www.gutenberg.org/ebooks/48482.

16. C. S. Lewis, *The Weight of Glory* (New York: Macmillan, 1949).

Chapter 4: Make Gratitude a Regular Practice

1. Robert A. Emmons and Michael E. McCullough, "Counting Blessings
    Versus Burdens: An Experimental Investigation of Gratitude and
    Subjective Well-Being in Daily Life," *Journal of Personality and Social
    Psychology* 84, no. 2 (February 2003): 377–89, https://greatergood
    .berkeley.edu/images/application_uploads/Emmons
    -CountingBlessings.pdf.

2. Randolph Wolf Shipon, "Gratitude: Effects on Perspectives and Blood
    Pressure of Inner-City African-American Hypertensive Patients"
    (PhD diss., Temple University, 2007).

3. Summer Allen, "The Science of Gratitude," *Greater Good Science Center*, May 2018, https://ggsc.berkeley.edu/images/uploads/GGSC -JTF_White_Paper-Gratitude-FINAL.pdf.

4. Gen. 2:18–19 (NIV).

5. Kenneth Blanchard and Spencer Johnson, *The One Minute Manager* (New York: William Morrow, 1982).

6. Kyle Benson, "The Magic Relationship Ratio, According to Science," *Gottman Institute*, October 4, 2017, https://www.gottman.com/blog /the-magic-relationship-ratio-according-science.

7. Blaise Pascal, *Pensées* (New York: Penguin Classics, 1995), 37.

8. Timothy D. Wilson et al., "Just Think: The Challenges of the Disengaged Mind," *Science* 345, no. 6192 (July 4, 2014): 75–77, https:// science.sciencemag.org/content/345/6192/75.

9. David Brooks, "The Structure of Gratitude," *New York Times*, July 28, 2015, https://www.nytimes.com/2015/07/28/opinion/david-brooks -the-structure-of-gratitude.html.

10. Daniel Simons and Christopher Chabris, "The Invisible Gorilla," 2010, http://www.theinvisiblegorilla.com/gorilla_experiment.html.

11. Paul Dolan, *Happiness by Design* (New York: Hudson Street Press, 2014).

Chapter 5: Learn to Forgive and Serve

1. Robert A. Emmons, *Thanks! How Practicing Gratitude Can Make You Happier* (Boston: Houghton Mifflin, 2008).

2. Kate Murphy, "The Futility of Vengeance," *New York Times*, February 7, 2015, https://www.nytimes.com/2015/02/08/sunday-review/the -futility-of-vengeance.html.

3. Murphy, "Futility of Vengeance."

4. Allen Kurzweil, *Whipping Boy: The Forty-Year Search for My Twelve-Year-Old Bully* (New York: HarperCollins, 2015).

5. Elahe Izadi, "The Powerful Words of Forgiveness Delivered to Dylann Roof by Victims' Relatives," *Washington Post*, June 19, 2015, https://www .washingtonpost.com/news/post-nation/wp/2015/06/19/hate-wont

-win-the-powerful-words-delivered-to-dylann-roof-by-victims
-relatives.

6. Charles Duhigg, *The Power of Habit: Why We Do What We Do in Life and Business* (New York: Random House, 2012).

7. Michael Gerson, "Trump's Toxic Temperament Should Disqualify Him from the Presidency," *Washington Post*, January 28, 2016, http://www.washingtonpost.com/opinions/trumps-toxic-temperament-should-disqualify-him-from-the-presidency/2016/01/28/1c1a7992-65e8-11e5-8965-0607e0e265ce_story.html.

8. Malcolm Gladwell, *David and Goliath* (New York: Little, Brown, 2013), chap. 8.

9. Matt. 18:21–22 (NKJV).

10. Eph. 4:32 (NKJV).

11. Matt. 16:25 (NKJV).

12. Ariel Knafo and Shalom H. Schwartz, "Accounting for Parent-Child Value Congruence: Theoretical Considerations and Empirical Evidence," *Cultural Transmission: Psychological, Developmental, Social, and Methodological Aspects* (Cambridge, MA: Cambridge Univ. Press, 2008), pp. 240–68.

13. Karen Caplovitz Barrett, Carolyn Zahn-Waxler, and Pamela M. Cole, "Avoiders vs. Amenders: Implications for the Investigation of Guilt and Shame During Toddlerhood," *Cognition and Emotion* 7, no. 6 (1993): 481–505.

14. V. J. Periyakoil, "Writing a 'Last Letter' When You're Healthy," *New York Times*, September 7, 2016, https://www.nytimes.com/2016/09/07/well/family/writing-a-last-letter-before-you-get-sick.html.

Chapter 6: Define Success and Failure for Yourself

1. Michael Lewis, *The New New Thing* (New York: W. W. Norton, 2000).

2. Belinda Luscombe, "Do We Need $75,000 a Year to Be Happy?," *Time*, September 6, 2010, http://content.time.com/time/magazine/article/0,9171,2019628,00.html.

3. Stephen M. Pollan and Mark Levine, *Die Broke: A Radical Four-Part Financial Plan* (New York: HarperBusiness, 1997).

4. Eric Barker, "Wondering What Happened to Your Class Valedictorian? Not Much, Research Shows," *Money*, May 18, 2017, http://money
.com/money/4779223/valedictorian-success-research-barking-up
-wrong.

5. Johannes Haushofer, "CV of Failures," https://www.princeton.edu
/~joha/Johannes_Haushofer_CV_of_Failures.pdf.

6. Prov. 23:7 (NKJV).

7. J. K. Rowling, "The Fringe Benefits of Failure, and the Importance of
Imagination," *Harvard Gazette*, June 5, 2008, https://news.harvard
.edu/gazette/story/2008/06/text-of-j-k-rowling-speech.

8. Clayton M. Christensen, "How Will You Measure Your Life?," *Harvard
Business Review*, July–August 2010, https://hbr.org/2010/07/how-will-you
-measure-your-life.

9. John 16:33 (NIV).

10. JoAnn Milivojevic, "Bounce Back from Adversity," *UCLA Health's
Healthy Years* 13, no. 2 (December 2016), https://universityhealthnews
.com/topics/stress-anxiety-topics/bounce-back-from-adversity.

11. American Psychological Association, "The Road to Resilience,"
https://www.apa.org/helpcenter/road-resilience.

12. Victor Goertzel and Mildred G. Goertzel, *Cradles of Eminence: A
Provocative Study of the Childhoods of Over 400 Famous Twentieth-
Century Men and Women* (New York: Little, Brown, 1962).

13. Mark D. Seery et al., "Whatever Does Not Kill Us: Cumulative Lifetime
Adversity, Vulnerability, and Resilience," *Journal of Personality and
Social Psychology* 99, no. 6 (December 2010): 1025–41, https://psycnet
.apa.org/buy/2010-21218-001.

14. Kelly McGonigal, "How to Make Stress Your Friend," TEDGlobal 2013,
https://www.ted.com/talks/kelly_mcgonigal_how_to_make_stress
_your_friend?language=en.

15. M. Scott Peck, *The Road Less Traveled* (New York: Simon & Schuster,
1978).

16. Carol Graham and Julia Ruiz Pozuelo, "Happiness, Stress, and
Age: How the U-Curve Varies across People and Places," *Journal of
Population Economics* 30, no. 1 (January 2017): 225–64, doi.org/10.1007
/s00148-016-0611-2.

Chapter 7: Invite Risk into Your Life

1. Margot Machol Bisnow, *Raising an Entrepreneur: 10 Rules for Nurturing Risk Takers, Problem Solvers, and Change Makers* (Oakland, CA: New Harbinger, 2016).

2. David Dobbs, "Restless Genes," *National Geographic*, January 2013, https://www.nationalgeographic.com/magazine/2013/01/restless-genes.

3. Dobbs, "Restless Genes."

4. Dobbs, "Restless Genes."

5. "Oldest Yoga Teacher: GWR Classics," https://www.youtube.com/watch?v=dZR7zB32vVs.

6. Robert Biswas-Diener and Todd B. Kashdan, "What Happy People Do Differently," *Psychology Today*, July 2, 2013, https://www.psychologytoday.com/us/articles/201307/what-happy-people-do-differently.

7. Studs Terkel, *Will the Circle Be Unbroken? Reflections on Death, Rebirth, and Hunger for a Faith* (New York: New Press, 2001).

8. Matt. 25:14–30 (NKJV).

9. Adam Grant, *Originals: How Non-Conformists Move the World* (New York: Penguin, 2016).

10. Jean Case, "The World Needs Us to Be Fearless," *Case Foundation*, February 28, 2012, https://casefoundation.org/blog/world-needs-us-fearless.

Chapter 8: Live an Integrated Life

1. Gillian Tett, *The Silo Effect: The Peril of Expertise and the Promise of Breaking Down Barriers* (New York: Simon & Schuster, 2015).

2. Tett, *The Silo Effect.*

3. Lauren Vesty, "Millennials Want Purpose over Paychecks. So Why Can't We Find It at Work?" *Guardian*, September 14, 2016, https://www.theguardian.com/sustainable-business/2016/sep/14/millennials-work-purpose-linkedin-survey.

4. Miya Tokumitsu, "In the Name of Love," *Jacobin*, January 12, 2014, https://www.jacobinmag.com/2014/01/in-the-name-of-love.

5. Gordon Marino, "A Life Beyond 'Do What you Love,'" *New York Times*, May 17, 2014, https://opinionator.blogs.nytimes.com/2014/05/17.

6. Steve Crabtree, "Worldwide, 13% of Employees Are Engaged at Work," *Gallup*, October 8, 2013, https://news.gallup.com/poll/165269 /worldwide-employees-engaged-work.aspx.

7. Gen. 1:10, 12, 18, 21, 25, 31 (NKJV).

8. Studs Terkel, *Working* (New York: Pantheon, 1974).

9. Robert E. Quinn and Anjan V. Thakor, "Creating a Purpose-Driven Organization," *Harvard Business Review*, July–August 2018, https://hbr .org/2018/07/creating-a-purpose-driven-organization.

10. David F. Larcker and Brian Tayan, "2018 CEO Activism Survey," Stanford Graduate School of Business and the Rock Center for Corporate Governance, https://www.gsb.stanford.edu/sites/gsb/files /publication-pdf/cgri-survey-2018-ceo-activism.pdf.

11. "Excerpts from the DealBook Conference," *New York Times*, November 14, 2017, https://www.nytimes.com/2017/11/14/business/dealbook/excerpts -dealbook-conference.html.

12. Erica Keswin, *Bring Your Human to Work* (New York: McGraw-Hill Education, 2018).

13. Nathaniel Koloc, "What Job Candidates Really Want: Meaningful Work," *Harvard Business Review*, April 18, 2013, https://hbr.org/2013/04 /what-job-candidates-really-wan.

14. "KPMG Purpose," KPMG Advisory, accessed November 21, 2019, https:// advisory.kpmg.us/insights/future-hr/future-hr-purpose-culture/kpmg -purpose.html.

15. Walter Isaacson, *Leonardo da Vinci* (New York: Simon & Schuster, 2017).

16. Marily Oppezzo and Daniel L. Schwartz, "Give Your Ideas Some Legs: The Positive Effect of Walking on Creative Thinking," *Journal of Experimental Psychology: Learning, Memory and Cognition* 40, no. 4 (April 2014): 1142–52, https://www.apa.org/pubs/journals/releases /xlm-a0036577.pdf.

17. Winston L. Churchill, *Painting as a Pastime* (London: Odhams Press, 1948).

18. Churchill, *Painting as a Pastime*.

19. Desmond Tutu and Mpho Tutu, *The Book of Forgiving: The Fourfold Path for Healing Ourselves and Our World* (San Francisco: HarperOne, 2014).

20. William Deresiewicz, "Don't Send Your Kid to the Ivy League: The Nation's Top Colleges Are Turning Our Kids into Zombies," *New Republic*, July 21, 2014, https://newrepublic.com/article/118747/ivy -league-schools-are-overrated-send-your-kids-elsewhere.

21. David Brooks, "Becoming a Real Person," *New York Times*, September 8, 2014, https://www.nytimes.com/2014/09/09/opinion/david-brooks -becoming-a-real-person.html.

22. Arthur Isak Applbaum, "Professional Detachment: The Executioner of Paris," *Harvard Law Review* 109, no. 2 (December 1995): 458–86 doi:10.2307/1341979.

23. W. H. Auden, *The Shield of Achilles* (New York: Random House, 1955), *Horae Canonicae*, "Sext," lines 1–10.

24. Andrew Steptoe, Angus Deaton, and Arthur A. Stone, "Subjective Wellbeing, Health, and Ageing," *The Lancet*, November 5, 2014, https:// www.thelancet.com/journals/lancet/article/PIIS0140-6736(13)61489-0 /fulltext.

25. Stewart D. Friedman, syllabus for "Executive Leadership," spring 2016, Wharton School of the University of Pennsylvania, https://syllabi -media.s3.amazonaws.com/prod/2016A-MGMT671001-86b50671.pdf.

Chapter 9: Leave a Legacy

1. Paula Span, "Death Be Not Decaffeinated: Over Cup, Groups Face Taboo," *New York Times*, June 16, 2013, https://newoldage.blogs.nytimes .com/2013/06/16/death-be-not-decaffeinated-over-cup-groups-face -taboo/.

2. Span, "Death Be Not Decaffeinated."

3. Jack London, *Jack London's Tales of Adventure*, ed. Irving Shepard (New York: Doubleday, 1956), p. vii.

4. Stephen R. Covey, *The 7 Habits of Highly Effective People* (New York: Free Press, 1989).

5. "Andrew Carnegie Becomes a Capitalist, 1856," Eyewitness to History, 2007, http://www.eyewitnesstohistory.com/carnegie.htm.

6. William Wilberforce, *William Wilberforce: Greatest Works* (Alachua, FL: Bridge-Logos, 2007), p. 10.

7. Wilberforce, *William Wilberforce: Greatest Works*, p. 17.

8. Dietrich Bonhoeffer, *Dietrich Bonhoeffer's Prison Poems*, ed. and trans. Edwin H. Robertson, 2nd ed. (Grand Rapids, MI: Zondervan, 2005), p. 41.

9. 1 Cor. 15:10 (NKJV).

10. Thomas Merton, *Thoughts in Solitude* (New York: Farrar, Straus and Cudahy, 1958).

Conclusion: Navigating Our Way

1. J. B. Phillips, *New Testament Christianity* (London: SCM Press, 1956; Eugene, OR: Wipf and Stock, 2012).